INVISIBLE HERO

TWO BOYS AND AN EXCITING TALE OF HONOR AND VALOR

Call Me No Hero
Retold for Young People

INVISIBLE HERO

TWO BOYS AND AN EXCITING TALE OF HONOR AND VALOR

Call Me No Hero
Retold for Young People

by
R. A. Sheats

Psalm 78 Ministries

www.psalm78ministries.com

Invisible Hero: Two Boys and an Exciting Tale of Honor and Valor

by R. A. Sheats

Published by:

Psalm 78 Ministries
P. O. Box 950
Monticello, FL 32345

www.psalm78ministries.com

ISBN: 978-1-720050810

Printed in the United States of America.

TABLE OF CONTENTS

To Jim Sledge,

whose selfless devotion to a fallen friend has kept the Boots Thomas story alive for over 70 years,

whose vision and dedication has motivated generation after generation of young people to study the heroes of the past,

and whose ability to see God's mercy in even the greatest of tragedies has been a never-ending source of inspiration to myself and others,

this book is respectfully dedicated

To the Parent

The history of Platoon Sergeant Ernest "Boots" Thomas has inspired people of all ages for generations. His small-town childhood, the unswerving dedication he brought to every task, and his heroic desire to protect his family and home—joined with the wartime fame of raising the Stars and Stripes on the bloody sands of Iwo Jima—make the story of Boots Thomas an exciting and inspiring tale for young and old alike.

As a young man who refused to glamorize his part in a justly historic battle and who bestowed all credit on his comrades instead of himself, Boots Thomas truly encapsulated the words of Solomon: "let another praise you, and not your own mouth" (Prov. 27:2). The history of his short life provides a stirring model for children of all ages. Thomas' diligence in even the little things, his responsibility in positions of authority, and his willing acceptance of the difficult tasks laid before him are all examples from which generations of children can learn. As his company commander Captain Dave Severance said of him on Iwo Jima: "I know of no more appropriate praise than to say that [Boots Thomas] was a credit to his parents who raised him."

Alongside the history of Sergeant Thomas flows the story of Jim Sledge, Thomas' closest friend. Raised in a little town in rural Florida, the two boys grew up together like brothers. When their paths diverged with college training and the coming of World War Two, they remained in contact through letters and visits. Boots joined the Marines and Jim enlisted in the Army Air Corps. After the war, Jim returned to Monticello alone. Boots' death on Iwo Jima at only twenty years of age could easily have been regarded as the last tragic scene in a tragically short life, but for Jim Sledge the solemn duty of honoring the memory of his fallen friend drove him to a lifetime of preserving the history of Boots' life and work and the lessons it provides to the rising generations. Jim's selfless dedication of keeping alive his friend's memory for over seven decades of life beautifully captures the truth of Solomon's words: "there is a friend who sticks closer than a brother" (Prov. 18:24).

Within *Invisible Hero* the history of Sergeant Boots Thomas and Jim Sledge (previously published under the title *Call Me No Hero*) has been condensed and rewritten for a younger audience. Though the story has been greatly abridged, the facts remain the same. It has been the author's intent throughout to preserve the historicity of the book for its younger readers.

All direct quotations have been drawn from letters and documents of the time as well as from personal interviews with the people involved in the story. Historical facts and events have been strictly adhered to, though most endnotes have been omitted in order to ease the flow of text. If a fuller listing of references or credits is desired, the reader is encouraged to examine the corresponding passages in *Call Me No Hero* (Psalm 78 Ministries, 2016).

"Honor your father and your mother, as the LORD *your God has commanded you, that your days may be long, and that it may be well with you in the land which the* LORD *your God is giving you."*
— Deuteronomy 5:16

CHAPTER ONE

A Boy Named Jim

Long ago, before most families owned refrigerators or televisions, a little boy lived in a small town in Florida called Monticello. His name was Jim and he was born on October 4, 1924.

Jim's real name was James Seymour Sledge, but everybody called him Jim. He grew up with his father and mother and his two older sisters on a little farm just outside of Monticello, where the family raised chickens and pigs.

When Jim was seven years old a big change came to his life when his father Lamar Sledge was elected county sheriff. As sheriff Lamar Sledge worked to protect the people of Monticello and Jefferson County. He and his deputies worked to keep the people safe and to stop criminals from breaking the law and hurting people. Being sheriff was a very important job.

When Mr. Sledge became sheriff he moved his family to the sheriff's quarters in Monticello which were located in the same building as the county jail. The family couldn't bring their farm animals with them now that they lived in town, and Jim missed the chickens, but he was excited to be living at the jailhouse.

Sheriff Sledge worked hard to protect the people of Monticello and to teach them what good laws were. But he also had to teach his family as well. Jim tried to be a good boy while he was growing up, but sometimes he was disobedient. Even though he knew he should always obey his parents, he sometimes gave in to temptation. One particularly tempting thing for Jim was a swimming pool at a neighbor's house not far from his own. When Jim was little he thought it would be fun to play around the swimming pool, but he hadn't yet learned how to swim. His father knew that if Jim played in the pool he would probably drown, so he told Jim: "Don't go over there and play around that swimming pool."

"Yes, sir!" Jim answered. But in his heart Jim still wanted to disobey, so he waited until he thought his father wasn't looking and then slipped away and crept over to the pool. Jim thought it would be fun, but he didn't realize that his father was watching him. Sheriff Sledge found him at the pool and sat him down for a talk.

"Well, son," his father said, "you've been disobedient, and you must be punished." Jim's father took him into the jail and locked him up in one of the cells.

It was quiet in the jail. There was a window in Jim's cell. He stood at the window and looked out. Soon he saw one of his friends walking down the street, so Jim decided to play a trick on him. He grabbed the bars in the window and called out to his friend: "Quick! Bring me something to eat! I'm on bread and water!"

After an hour or two Sheriff Sledge unlocked the cell door and let Jim go free. Jim didn't mind being locked up. He was glad he didn't get a spanking for being disobedient, because he knew he deserved it. He also knew he should never play around that swimming pool again.

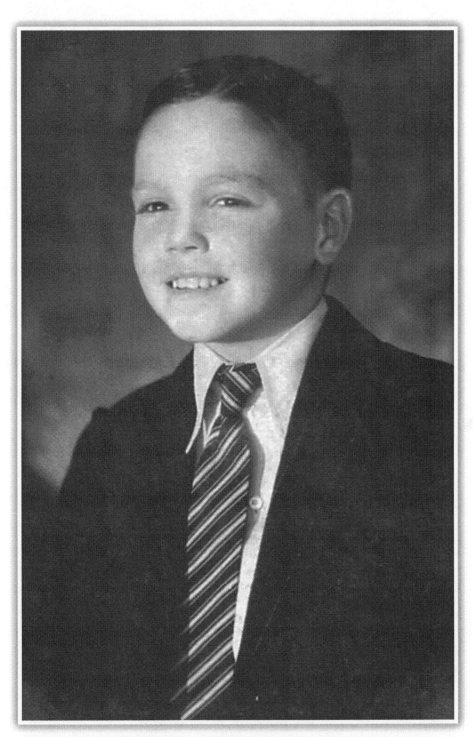

Jim Sledge when he was 10 years old

CHAPTER TWO

A Very Sad Night

Jim enjoyed living in Monticello beside the jail. But suddenly one day his life changed forever. When he only nine years old his father was called out on a mission one night in February of 1934. Sheriff Lamar took a deputy with him when he went. It was getting late, so Jim was sent to bed before his father came home.

While Jim was asleep, Sheriff Lamar and his deputy ran into some trouble. A gunfight broke out, and both Sheriff Lamar and his deputy were shot. The deputy died instantly and Sheriff Lamar was rushed to a hospital.

Jim was scared when he heard that his father was in the hospital. He hoped his daddy would be able to come home soon, but while Sheriff Lamar was in the hospital complications set in. In the 1930's doctors didn't have access to antibiotics like they do today, and two weeks after the gunfight Jim's father died.

Monticello was very sorry to lose their sheriff. They loved Lamar Sledge and were very sad when he died. Almost a thousand people gathered for the funeral. Many people came from all over the state to attend, bringing flowers and wreaths to show how much they would miss Sheriff Sledge. Everyone tried to comfort Jim and his mother and sisters, but it was a sad time for little Jim. He missed his daddy very much.

Jim had an uncle named Theodore Sledge, but people called him Teddy. He lived in Georgia, but when he heard that Sheriff Lamar had been shot, he came down to Florida to be

Jim's parents, Lamar and Rena Sledge

Uncle Teddy Sledge

with the family.

After Jim's father died, Uncle Teddy wanted to do everything he could to help take care of Jim since he didn't have a father anymore. When summer came, Uncle Teddy invited Jim to come live with him for a few months in Georgia. He said he would be a father to Jim and would take care of him as if he were his own son.

Uncle Teddy was a soldier. When he was a young man he fought in World War One. With many other Americans he had sailed to Europe and fought in France. He had been part of a tank battalion. Tanks were a new invention in World War One, and Teddy Sledge was very excited to be able to use

Tank knocking down a tree during World War One

them.

When the war ended, Uncle Teddy came home. In 1934 he was stationed in Atlanta, Georgia at an army base. For the summer of 1934 Jim stayed with him and learned a little about army life.

When fall came Jim went home to his mother and sisters in Monticello. They couldn't live at the jail anymore because the town now had a new sheriff, so his mother found another home for them a few blocks away. Jim moved into his new home on Pearl Street and began getting ready because school was about to begin. With a new school year coming, Jim wondered what life would be like and what new friends he would make.

CHAPTER THREE

Finding a Friend

In 1932 a new family moved into the town of Monticello. Ernest and Martha Thomas were from Tampa, Florida but decided to move to Monticello because they wanted a quiet place to raise their children. Ernest Thomas was a traveling salesman with the Florida Pipe Supply Company.

When Mr. Thomas was a little boy he often wore boots to school. He liked wearing boots, and soon all his classmates called him "Boots." He didn't mind at all. He liked the name. When he grew up people still called him Boots.

Ernest and Martha Thomas had three children. Their oldest child was born on March 10, 1924 and was named after his father Ernest, but nobody called him Ernest. They all called him Boots Junior or just Boots. He had two younger siblings, Jean and Jack.

When the Thomas children moved to Monticello they didn't have any friends in town, but little Boots hoped he would make friends quickly. He and his family lived on a quiet street called Pearl Street, and other little boys also lived on the street. One of them was Jim Sledge, who lived just across the road. Before long Boots and Jim met and became close friends.

Ten-year-old Boots and nine-year-old Jim spent most of their time together over the fall of 1934. Then, in September of that year, a hurricane struck Monticello. The clouds were so thick that it looked like nighttime in the middle of the afternoon. Gusts of wind shrieked through the town and rain poured down in torrents. Boots and Jim and their

Boots Thomas *(left)* **with his mother and siblings**

families huddled anxiously inside their houses while the storm passed through, ripping up trees by their roots and smashing buildings and vehicles. It was a frightening time for the entire town. The storm cut off the electricity to the city, so Boots and his family used candles to be able to see each other.

When morning finally arrived, the storm had passed, but Monticello was a disaster. Tree limbs and debris covered the roads and yards. Roofs had been blown off of some of the houses, and many buildings were severely damaged. Living through the hurricane was a scary and an exciting time for Boots. He wrote about it in his journal:

September 4, 1934
Hurricane hit here about three o'clock. One of our big trees fell down and blocked the road. Worst storm Monticello ever had. Wind blowing 70 miles per hour. Lights went out. Used candles. Stopped about midnight. The whole town is a wreck. All of our trees blew down and the yard is full of limbs.

After the hurricane passed and the trees were cleaned up Boots and Jim got together and found something new to do. Neither boy owned a bicycle, but they both wanted to learn how to ride, so they borrowed their neighbor's bicycle and taught themselves to ride.

Learning to ride a bike with a friend is always fun. But, even though Jim was only ten years old, he knew that he couldn't spend all his time riding bicycles. Since his father was dead Jim needed to help provide for his mother and sisters.

In Tallahassee, a city not far from Monticello, the House of Representatives met. The House was a group of men who were part of the state's government and who met together to conduct business. Jim's father had been a representative before he became sheriff. Now it was Jim's turn to help the state legislature. In 1935 he became a page. A page's job was to help the representatives by running errands for them and getting them anything they might need. Many of the representatives were friends of Jim's father. They were happy that Jim had come to the legislature, too.

Jim was paid $4.00 a day while he was a page. Four dollars was a large amount of money in 1935 and Jim was very excited to earn it. The House of Representatives met for two months, during which time Jim earned $240. He brought the money home to his mother and was glad that he could help her in this way.

Occasionally when Jim ran errands for the representatives they gave him a tip. Sometimes he would receive a nickel and sometimes he would receive a dime. Jim's mother let him keep all the tip money he received. Jim saved his money until he and Boots Thomas could get together. Then they would walk down the street to their favorite store. It was run by a man that all the children in town called Candy Jones.

Candy Jones got his name because he sold many different kinds of candy at his store. Mr. Jones was a short, white-haired man who loved children. Often when Jim and Boots bought candies from him Mr. Jones would give them extra. He always liked to have children come into his store. All the children loved him, too.

CHAPTER FOUR

An Exciting Climb

When fall arrived the two boys went to school together in Monticello. Boots was diligent with his studies and also worked with other students who needed help. When his class chose a president, they elected Boots. He looked after the class and also helped his teachers whenever they needed anything.

Even though he was still a child, Boots' parents had taught him to be responsible. He always tried to listen to his teachers and help the other students, but he also liked to have fun.

During their school years Boots and Jim spent time discussing what they would do when they grew up. Boots planned to become an aeronautical engineer. Jim decided he'd do the same thing. The boys then decided they would go to South America to make their fortune.

"We'll make a million dollars and then come back," Jim said.

But, before they could go to South America, the boys needed to learn Spanish. They decided that the best thing to do would be to go to Cuba and learn the language. But going to Cuba cost money, so Boots and Jim started saving their pennies. They gathered glass coca-cola bottles from around town and brought them back to the factory. The factory paid two cents apiece for the bottles. The boys hoped they could make enough money from the bottles to go to Cuba after they graduated, but soon they realized that they'd need a lot more money than they could earn from gathering bottles.

Getting enough money to go to Cuba would be difficult, so Boots and Jim began learning Spanish right away. When they wrote letters to each other, they signed them *tú amigo* (which means *your friend* in Spanish). Boots had a good memory and memorized the Spanish words very quickly.

Because they were best friends, Boots and Jim loved to do everything together. One day when Boots got a new camera he rushed over to Jim's house to show him his new possession. He wanted to try the camera out, so the boys went for a walk around town to try to find something to take a picture of.

While they were walking Jim looked across the street at the city's water tower. It was the tallest structure in town.

"I wonder if we can see Lake Miccosukee off the top of that water tower?" Jim asked.

Boots thought it was a great idea to climb the tower, but he knew that they weren't allowed on the tower without permission. He suggested that they ask the city mayor, Richard Simpson, for permission to climb. Jim agreed, and off they went to the mayor's office.

Mayor Simpson was busily working at his desk when the two boys entered his office. Boots and Jim excitedly explained that they'd like to take some pictures from the top of the water tower and asked permission to climb it. Mr. Simpson was thinking about his work and didn't really listen to what the boys were saying. When they asked for permission, he said it was fine with him as long as they were careful.

Boots and Jim raced back to the water tower and prepared to climb the steep ladder that led to its top. Boots brought a rope with him and tied one end to himself and the other to Jim in case one of them fell. Then they carefully climbed to the top of the tower.

The view from the top of the water tower was beautiful. The boys were so high in the air that they could see the entire town stretched out under them. Boots took a picture of the courthouse with his new camera and he and Jim excitedly

Monticello water tower

watched the cars and people far down below them.

While they were watching the town, Boots and Jim didn't realize that the people in town were watching them, too. Someone saw them on the water tower and was afraid that they would fall off and hurt themselves, so they called the fire department. The firefighters quickly rushed over to the water tower and called up to the surprised boys.

"What do you all think you're doing?" the firemen asked.

"Just taking pictures," the boys responded.

The fireman weren't very happy with the boys' answer and told them that they weren't allowed on the water tower.

Boots and Jim carefully climbed back down to the ground and explained to the firemen: "We went and asked Mr. Simpson and he said it was alright."

**A picture Boots took from
the top of the water tower**

CHAPTER FIVE

Time to Grow Up

Time passed pleasantly in Monticello. When the summer of 1939 arrived, Boots was fifteen years old. He looked forward to the long quiet days he would spend fishing over the summer months. A little stream ran by the road two miles from his house and Boots loved to fish in it. Sometimes he and Jim would go fishing and sometimes Boots would take his little brother Jack instead. He and Jack liked to sit on the bank with their poles in the water and spend the day talking. They never caught many fish, but Jack always loved these special days with his big brother.

In August of that year Boots' father Ernest Thomas became ill. He went to see the doctor and discovered that something was wrong with his heart. The doctor told Mr. Thomas that he needed to stay in bed and rest or else he would die. Boots' father obeyed the doctor and for six long weeks he rested, hoping to get well. Boots was frightened to see his father so sick. His little brother and sister Jack and Jean were very scared, too. That summer they spent a lot of time visiting with their father while he lay in bed.

Boots' mother hoped that her husband would get better quickly after he had a long rest, but Mr. Thomas didn't get well. On October 24th, very unexpectedly, he died.

Boots was stunned. He was only fifteen years old and could hardly believe that his father had died. Friends and relatives came to comfort the family, but Boots went to his room and sat down to think.

Grave of Mr. Thomas, Boots' father

Jim Sledge visited Boots on the day his father died. He found Boots in his bedroom by himself. The boys talked together.

Since his father was dead, Boots knew that he was responsible for his family.

"You know," he told Jim, "I'm the man of the house now. I've got to take care of this family." Even though he was only fifteen, Boots knew it was time to grow up.

After his father died, Boots and his mother and siblings didn't have any source of income. Mrs. Thomas, Boots' mother, began looking for work and Boots also began working at the local A & P grocery store each afternoon after school.

When Boots was growing up in the 1930's grocery stores were a little different than they are today. When a person wanted groceries, he would go to the store and give his list of groceries to the clerk. Then the clerk would gather everything he wanted and add up all the prices on an adding machine. Crackers and potatoes were stored in large bins or barrels. Candies were sorted into glass jars on the counter. Sometimes there was even a checkerboard set up for people to play checkers while they waited.

Boots worked so diligently at the A & P grocery

store that Mr. Cooper, the owner of another grocery store in Monticello called the Suwannee store, offered Boots a job at his store and promised to pay him more than what the A & P was paying him. Boots went to work for Mr. Cooper and became assistant manager of the store even though he was still only a teenager. Some days Mr. Cooper didn't even come into the store to check up on it. Boots knew that he needed to be very responsible and work hard to manage the store well, and Mr. Cooper trusted him. Because Boots was faithful in even the little things, Mr. Cooper knew that he would be faithful in the bigger task of running the entire store alone.

Boots only worked in the afternoon on school days, but on Saturdays he worked all day long. Sometimes Jim would work on Saturdays, too. He got paid twenty-five cents an hour and worked from six in the morning until nine o'clock at night.

Old-time grocery store

Saturday was the biggest day for the grocery stores. All the farmers came in from out of town and brought their produce to sell. They also came to purchase their groceries for the week. Monticello filled up on that day, with people everywhere. The boys had to work hard to assist all the customers and look after the store.

Soon after Boots' father died his great-grandfather came to live with the family. James Lafayette Turrentine was Mrs. Thomas' grandfather. As a young man he had fought in the War Between the States. He was from Alabama and served as a private in the infantry. But now he was 94 years old and needed someone to live with.

Boots and his family were glad to have Grandfather Turrentine come to live with them. The children all loved him and were surprised at how strong and agile he was even as an old man. Grandfather Turrentine quickly earned their respect and became a cherished member of the family.

Both the Thomas and Sledge families attended the local Baptist church in Monticello. Boots had attended the church since he was a child, and not long after his father died he made a public profession of faith and asked to be baptized.

During Boots' years at high school his mother kept looking for work. She needed to find a job so that she could provide for her family since her husband had died. At last she found a job in the nearby city of Tallahassee.

First Baptist Church of Monticello

CHAPTER SIX

A Dangerous Man

While Boots and Jim were growing up in Monticello, big changes were happening in other parts of the world. In Germany a new leader had risen and was trying to change his country. He was called a *chancellor,* and his name was Adolf Hitler. Mr. Hitler was a wicked man, but when he first became the leader many people didn't know what he was like. He said that he wanted to save Germany and protect its people. Many of the Germans believed him. They thought he would help their nation and would give them better jobs and a better country. Mr. Hitler promised he would help and the people didn't know that he was lying, but soon they would find out that they were wrong.

Mr. Hitler had a plan. He wanted to make Germany bigger by attacking other countries and stealing all their land from them. He pretended that he was a friend of the other countries, but he really only wanted to deceive them so he could send in his armies and navy and destroy them.

When the German people found out that Mr. Hitler wanted to go to war and steal from other countries, they were surprised. Some of the Germans opposed him and said that what he was doing was wrong. Other people decided that they would help him because they hoped that they would get rich if they helped with Mr. Hitler's war.

Because Mr. Hitler wanted to start a war, he had to do many things that were against the law. He was afraid that people might try to stop him because he was doing things that

Adolf Hitler, chancellor of Germany

were wrong, so he told the people that he was allowed to do anything he wanted because he was the leader of Germany. He said: "I was responsible for the fate of the German people, and I thereby became the supreme judge of the German people."[1]

Mr. Hitler tried to make people believe that he didn't need to obey the law because he was a leader, but he was wrong. Even the greatest leaders and the highest rulers must obey the law. No one is allowed to do something wrong, even if they think it is a good thing to do. People must always obey the law and do what is right, even when they're big and important people.

When Mr. Hitler began to make his plans, he decided to get rid of anyone who wasn't helpful to him. He was a very wicked man, and he decided to kill many, many people. He told his nation that people who were very sick or who had developmental disabilities or physical deformities should all be murdered. He even told people to kill little children. He believed that only the strongest people should be allowed to live.

Mr. Hitler was very, very wrong, but he still tried to make people believe him. He tried to teach all the children of Germany to obey him instead of obeying their parents. He told them that they shouldn't follow what the Bible said. He wanted everyone to follow him. He wanted them to treat him like a god. He told them: "I am freeing man from the restraints of intelligence . . . from the dirty and degraded self-mortifications called conscience and morality. . . . The world can be ruled only by fear."[2]

Soon a war started in Europe. Mr. Hitler attacked many small countries and defeated them. Russia joined with him and became an ally or a friend of Germany. Japan also joined Mr. Hitler. But England and France told Mr. Hitler that he had to stop attacking other countries. When he didn't stop, they declared war on him. All of Europe began fighting.

The Philippines

CHAPTER SEVEN

An Adventure
in the Philippines

In 1940 Jim's Uncle Teddy Sledge was transferred from Georgia to the Philippines, a group of islands off the coast of southeast Asia. The United States Army had many men stationed in the Philippines and sent Uncle Teddy to help with the work that needed to be done there.

Uncle Teddy was a major in the army. Before he left for the Philippines Major Teddy Sledge visited Jim's mother and asked if he could take Jim with him. The army wanted him to stay in the Philippines for two years and Major Sledge didn't want to leave Jim without a father for that long.

Mrs. Sledge was sad to think of parting with her son for two years, but she knew that it would be good for Jim to spend that time with Uncle Teddy.

Jim was excited when he heard he was going to the Philippines. The long ocean voyage and life in the Philippine islands halfway around the world sounded like a grand adventure. Jim eagerly packed his bags and said goodbye to his family and friends. He and Boots promised to write each other. Then Jim and his uncle left for South Carolina, where they boarded the ship that would take them to the Philippines by way of the Panama Canal.

The Panama Canal was a canal built across Panama in Central America that allowed ships to sail from the Atlantic to the Pacific Ocean without having to go all the way around

A battleship passing through the Panama Canal

the tip of South America. Traveling through the canal was an exciting time for Jim. After the ship made it through the canal it stopped at San Francisco in California for a day or two before setting sail westward toward the Philippines.

Jim's grandmother Mrs. Hattie Sledge and his aunt Jerry traveled with him and Major Sledge to the Philippines. Grandmother Sledge was 80 years old, but she still looked forward to the voyage across the ocean and her time in the Philippines with her family. While she sailed across the Pacific she rose early each morning to watch the beautiful sunrises across the water. She wrote:

May 14th
Another perfect day. Sea very calm. Ted and I got up at the first streaks of day to see the pretty sunrise. We stood on deck for an hour looking at God's beauty,

Jim on his way to the Philippines with his Uncle Teddy and his aunt and grandmother

and I can stand, look, and think for hours.

Just as the sun was coming up over the water, Ted said, "I will go and call Jim. I want him to see it, too."

Jim enjoyed his trip across the ocean and stood excitedly on deck when the Philippine islands finally came into view. Palm trees and long white, sparkling beaches met his eyes. Everything looked strange and mysterious.

Jim and his uncle and family were stationed near Manila, the capital of the Philippines. Major Sledge was assigned to the 57th Infantry at Fort McKinley. While they were there Aunt Jerry and Grandmother Sledge looked after the house and Jim began school in Manila. Every morning an army truck picked him up and drove him into Manila for school.

Life in the Philippines was full of interesting adventures for Jim. When he wasn't in school he explored the island and played with the other children at Fort McKinley. He missed his family in Monticello and wrote them letters. He also wrote Boots and told him all about his new life.

Major Sledge was stationed at Fort McKinley, but sometimes he went on short trips to other places on the islands for his army work. He liked to take Jim with him on these trips. Once they went to Bataan, a peninsula located across the bay from Manila. The army needed another training facility for the soldiers and put Major Sledge in charge of building it. Jim stayed in Bataan for a few days while his uncle worked on the new facility.

One morning while they were in Bataan Uncle Teddy woke Jim up early and took him outside. Across the water was a little island called Corregidor. There was another army base on Corregidor, and every morning the soldiers there raised the American flag.

Corregidor was a long way from Bataan, but Jim could faintly see the army base in the distance. And, as the sun crept over the horizon in the early morning light, Jim and his uncle stood quietly and watched as the flag was slowly raised.

"You know, Jim," Uncle Teddy told him, "there are some things in life you'll die for, and that's one of them."

Jim didn't say anything, but he knew what his uncle meant. That American flag represented freedom. It represented safety and protection for himself and his family. If an enemy attacked his country and tried to steal his family's freedom and safety, Jim knew that his Uncle Teddy would fight that enemy to protect his family and his home, even if he died fighting them.

Jim knew that at that moment many men in Europe were fighting a war to protect their homes and families from their enemy Mr. Hitler. Battles were being fought there and many people were dying. Jim didn't like to think about people dying. His father was already dead, and he didn't want any more of his family or friends to die. And, as the sun silently rose in the peaceful morning sky, Jim stood and watched the flag on Corregidor and hoped that war would never come to his country.

Jim Sledge and Boots Thomas, summer of 1941

CHAPTER EIGHT

Summer and Snakes

Back in Monticello Boots Thomas was finishing up high school while his friend Jim was in the Philippines. When Boots finished school he planned to attend college to study aeronautical engineering. His mother Mrs. Thomas knew that Boots would be very good at engineering, and she encouraged her son in his studies. She loved her children very much, and throughout their childhood she and her husband had worked carefully to train Boots and his siblings. Boots knew that studying and learning at school was important, but he also knew that his mother was more concerned about his character than his studies. She wanted her son to become a good man, not just a smart man. Boots thought about this when he prepared to go to college, and he tried to remember everything his mother had taught him.

No colleges near Monticello offered a degree in aeronautical engineering, so Boots applied to a college in Angola, Indiana called Tri-State College. He chose this college because their training program for engineering was a fast-paced program that would allow Boots to graduate with his degree in in a much shorter time than most colleges. Boots was happy to think that he wouldn't need to be away from home for very long.

Boots sent in an application to Tri-State College and asked to be accepted into their engineering program. Mr. Jones, the principal of Boots' high school in Monticello, also sent a letter to Tri-State to let them know what kind of a boy

Jim and Boots, 1941

Boots was. He wrote about Boots: "He had the best possible home training which has resulted in fine character. I can truthfully recommend Ernest as the most promising graduate of Monticello High School."

The reviewing board at Tri-State read Boots' application and Mr. Jones' letter and wrote to say that they would accept Boots as a student. Boots looked forward to beginning his engineering training in September.

In May of 1941 Boots graduated from high school and spent the summer working at the Suwannee store in Monticello. Early in the summer he also received very exciting news: Jim Sledge was coming home from the Philippines!

But why was Jim coming home? Major Sledge had planned to keep his adopted son with him in the Philippines for two years. But when the summer of 1941 came Uncle Teddy began to worry about Jim.

The Philippine islands are located off the coast of Asia. Not far from them is the country of Japan. When Mr. Hitler began his war in Europe, Japan became friends with Mr. Hitler. Close to the same time the Japanese started a war in China and began training Japanese men to become soldiers. The United States didn't like what Japan was doing, and soon an argument started between the two countries. The Japanese got angry, and America got angry, too.

When Major Sledge saw that the Japanese and the Americans were arguing, he knew that the Japanese might attack the Americans. If they did, there would be fighting in the Philippines. Many men would fight, and many men would die. Major Sledge didn't want Jim to stay in the Philippines if a war was coming, so he sent him and his grandmother and aunt back home to America. He wanted them to be safe in case the Japanese attacked.

Jim's mother and sisters were very happy to see him again when he arrived home in Monticello. They had missed him while he was in the Philippines and were glad that he was home safely.

Boots was excited to see Jim, too. He and Jim spent days talking about the Philippines and about what had happened in Monticello while Jim was gone.

During the summer the two boys spent a lot of time together. Watermelon season came in June. Both boys loved the sweet, juicy fruit. They helped bring in the harvest and helped to eat it, too. Sweet corn also became ripe over the summer months. When that happened families in Monticello held corn-husking parties. Boots and Jim were invited to the parties and helped gather the corn from the fields and husk it so that it could be put up or eaten. Husking corn was always a messy, sticky job, but it was fun, especially when family and friends joined together in the work.

Summer days were also good for bike riding. Boots and Jim owned their own bicycles now and enjoyed long rides through the country. Sometimes they would go fishing or exploring. One day they stopped at a stream and decided to follow it up through the woods to find the source of the water.

Crickets chirped their melodies as Boots and Jim walked through the woods following the stream. Mosquitoes whined around them and the boys slapped the insects away while they continued their journey. Boots led the way and Jim followed.

The trees around the stream's edge hid the sun from view and created pockets of shade on the warm sunny afternoon. Suddenly, as Jim walked, he saw something hidden in one of the patches of shade.

"Boots," he called, "I think I see a snake!"

Boots stopped and looked where Jim was pointing. There on the ground lying beside the stream was a large water moccasin, a big black venomous snake. Boots knew the snake was very dangerous and decided that he ought to kill it. He carefully cut himself a stick and quickly killed the snake with it.

After the snake was dead Boots and Jim carried it back through the woods to their bicycles. They were very careful with the snake because they knew that a moccasin's venom can kill a person even after the snake is dead.

When they reached their bicycles Boots tied the snake to the back of his bike. Then he and Jim rode back into town and circled around the courthouse to show the townspeople their trophy. They were very excited that they had killed the snake.

When Boots and Jim's mothers heard what they had done, however, they told the boys that playing with snakes was a very foolish thing to do. Boots and Jim learned that day that they should always leave snake-killing to adults.

The summer days of 1941 were special days for Boots and Jim. But, when fall arrived, Boots said farewell to his family and friends and journeyed north to Indiana to begin college. Jim also prepared to go back to high school to finish up his schooling. The two boys said goodbye and looked forward to when they would see each other over Christmas break.

Boots Thomas as a freshman in college

CHAPTER NINE

War is Coming!

In September of 1941 Boots Thomas left Monticello and headed north to Angola, Indiana to begin studying at Tri-State College. Indiana was the furthest from home that Boots had ever been. Everything in Indiana was strange and new.

Boots found a place to stay in a boarding house owned by a woman named Mrs. Truesdale. Mrs. Truesdale rented rooms to students at Tri-State. She was happy to have Boots stay with her because he was such a responsible young man. He was only seventeen years old, but she told him that he was the best boarder she ever had.

Boots was glad to find a nice place to stay at Mrs. Truesdale's boarding house, but he was surprised to learn how expensive everything was away from home. He had to pay rent for his room in the boardinghouse, and he also had to pay someone to wash his laundry every week for him. Mrs. Thomas, Boots' mother, knew that living at college would be expensive for her son. Not only did he need money for his lodging and laundry, but he also needed money for food. Boots didn't have a job in Indiana, so Mrs. Thomas mailed him a check every month to pay for his living expenses.

Boots was very grateful for his mother's financial help. Sometimes Mrs. Thomas also sent extra money for Boots to spend. "Thanks a lot for the dollar," Boots would write her.[3]

The classes at Tri-State College were exciting for Boots, but they were hard as well. In his first semester he studied chemistry, mechanical drawing, college algebra, and English.

Work at college was much trickier than it had been during high school. Mechanical drawing was the most difficult course for Boots. "I'm still studying awful hard," he wrote his mother. "In fact I hardly have a chance to write. It seems like the harder and longer I work on my mechanical drawing, the worse I get."[4]

Working so hard at his classes could get discouraging for Boots, but he knew that the material he was learning was important for him to know so that he could be a good aeronautical engineer. He studied diligently even though it was difficult for him. Each day at school his teachers assigned homework for the students to finish at home. Boots carefully worked through all his homework each night even though his teachers never asked to see whether he had finished it or not. Boots knew that he needed to do the right thing even if no one was watching him. "I do every bit of my homework every night," he wrote to his mother. "But my teachers don't check on it."[5]

The weather in Indiana turned cold quickly after Boots began college there. His mother mailed him an overcoat to help keep him warm during the coming winter. She knew that it would start snowing there even while it was still hot in Florida.

From college Boots wrote his mother every few days. He missed everyone in Monticello very much and was always excited to get letters from them. "Tell everybody hello for me and write real often because I like to get letters," he wrote his mother.[6] Sometimes he worried about his family, too. In October of 1941 another hurricane struck Florida. It hit Tallahassee where Mrs. Thomas was living, but nobody was hurt. Boots was glad to hear that everyone was alright.

Boots made many friends while he was at college. One of his classmates came from Mexico. Martes Gonzalez was his name. Martes didn't speak English very well, so Boots helped him learn the language. In return Martes helped Boots practice his Spanish. The boys enjoyed learning from each other and Boots wished that Jim could also come learn Spanish from Martes.

Soon Boots' first semester at college was almost over. During the final days of November Boots checked the calendar and saw that he only had a few more weeks of college left before he could go home for Christmas. But, while he was getting ready to go home, the Japanese were getting ready to go to war against America.

After arguing with America for many years, Japan finally decided that the best way to get what they wanted was to go to war. On December 7, 1941 they attacked the American naval yard at Pearl Harbor in Hawaii. Many men died during the attack, and America knew that it would need to fight the Japanese to protect itself.

The Japanese also attached the Philippines and bombed the American bases there. When news of the attacks reached the United States, Jim worried about his Uncle Teddy who was still living in the Philippines. He hoped that he wouldn't be

Japanese bombers over Corregidor

killed by the Japanese.

Less than two weeks after the Japanese bombed Pearl Harbor Boots finished his semester at Tri-State and returned home to his family in Florida. Now that America was at war, Boots decided that he should stop studying aeronautical engineering and instead join the military service so that he could defend his country and family. Boots talked about this to his mother.

"I've got to go to war, even if I am only 17," he told her. "I can't stand it any longer. I've got to fight."[7]

Mrs. Thomas knew that Boots wanted to help protect her and his family and country, but she didn't want him to go to war. She was afraid that he might get killed. Her husband had died only two years ago, and she didn't want to lose her oldest son as well.

Boots asked for permission to go to war, but his mother told him no. She asked him to wait a little longer. Boots wanted to fight the Japanese, but he knew that he needed to obey his mother even when it was difficult to do so. When she told him he couldn't go to war, he obeyed her.

Mrs. Thomas and her children celebrated Christmas in Florida. Then, when January of 1942 arrived, Boots said goodbye to his family and headed back to Indiana to begin his new college classes.

Getting back to school was a big change for Boots. It had been warm in Florida over Christmas, but when he arrived back in Indiana the temperature was 11° below zero. "I mean that is really cold!" Boots wrote his mother.[8] He was very thankful for the overcoat and sweaters that she had given him.

Boots' new classes were even more difficult than his old ones had been. He worked hard studying but sometimes he still didn't get all his work done. He was glad when the end of the semester came and he could go home to Florida.

CHAPTER TEN

Joining the Marines

On the Philippine islands American soldiers fought for many months to defend themselves against the attacking Japanese. The Americans fought bravely, but they were running out of food, and no supplies from the United States could reach them.

General Jonathan Wainwright commanded the American troops in the Philippines. After five long months of bitter fighting, General Wainwright knew that his men couldn't fight any longer. In May of 1942 he wrote to President Roosevelt in Washington:

> We are now overwhelmingly assaulted by Japanese troops. There is a limit of human endurance and that limit has long since been past. Without prospect of relief I feel it is my duty to my country and to my gallant troops to end this useless effusion of blood and human sacrifice.[9]

General Wainwright knew that America wasn't sending any fresh soldiers to help the men in the Philippines fight. Without more help the Americans in the islands couldn't continue the battle. They had retreated to Corregidor, but they were surrounded by the Japanese and were running out of food. If they didn't surrender, they would all die. General Wainwright knew they only had one option left, so with a heavy heart he ordered his men to lower the American flag on

Americans surrendering on Corregidor

Corregidor and raise the white flag of surrender.

As soon as the fighting ended 70,000 American and Filipino troops surrendered as prisoners of war to Japan. Jim's Uncle Teddy was one of them. He would remain a prisoner of the Japanese unless American forces could win the war and rescue him.

The United States was stunned at the loss of so many American soldiers. The people of America knew that many more soldiers would be needed to win the war against Japan and bring their captured countrymen home. Across the nation young men joined the military forces and prepared to play their part in the defense of their homeland.

American poster from WWII

Recruits training at Parris Island

Now that Boots had finished his college work for the spring he again asked his mother if he could sign up to fight in the war. This time Mrs. Thomas said yes, and Boots excitedly enlisted in the Marine Corps.

At first the Marine Corps wouldn't accept Boots. He was colorblind and therefore couldn't pass his visual test. But Boots quickly memorized the colorblind chart and was finally accepted and ordered to Parris Island in South Carolina for training. Saying goodbye to his family and friends, Boots again left Florida and headed north in the final days of May 1942.

The training center of Parris Island trained thousands of young men to become Marines. When Boots Thomas arrived he wrote a quick note to his mother to let her know that he'd made it safely. Then he began his training as a Marine.

Life at Parris Island was very busy for the men and boys who were trained there. Each recruit was instructed in self-discipline and was taught how to obey orders. He also learned how to march and to handle a rifle.

Physical training was another big part of a young Marine's life. Boots had gotten a little out of shape during his time in college, but his training at Parris Island fixed that. He wrote his mother: "Right now I have blisters on my feet, my face is sun-burned, and every muscle in my body is sore, but I am rapidly hardening up and getting in good shape."[10]

Boots and the other young Marines got up each morning at five o'clock and worked until ten o'clock at night. Life during training was hard and wasn't much fun at all, but Boots didn't mind. He wrote his mother:

> We are all looking forward to leaving here. Nobody likes it here because you are practically a prisoner for six weeks. But we know we have to have this training to become a Marine, so we don't mind it.[11]

During his time in training Boots learned how to use a bayonet and how to throw grenades. He learned how to read maps and how to work together with a group of men to accomplish a goal. Boots had even more to learn during his Marine training than he had had to learn during his college studies. But he knew that it was important for him to learn what his drill instructor taught him, so he studied diligently.

On Parris Island Boots was assigned to a group of 64 men called a *platoon*. He worked and lived with these men throughout his training period. The platoon was trained by a drill sergeant. The drill sergeant was very strict with his men. He required them all to learn to do exactly what he told them. Remembering everything was sometimes difficult, but Boots didn't mind it being hard. He enjoyed learning because he knew that when he finished his training he would be ready to help defend his family and his home against the Japanese.

Boots wanted his mother to understand what his life was like on Parris Island, but it was difficult to explain everything he and the other recruits were learning and practicing. He wrote her on June 23, 1942:

> There is no way in the world for me to tell you how much we do here. We drill, practice landing parties, have bayonet drill, do physical exercise with the rifle, clean our rifles, clean the barracks, and besides all that, have as much to memorize and learn as I ever had in college or school. The responsibility on one man in the Marine Corps is more than I ever dreamed of.[12]

Boots' drill instructor, Sergeant Rogers, was responsible for training the 64 men of his platoon. For the first week of their training Sergeant Rogers watched Boots. He saw that the young Floridian was eager to learn and was quick to follow instructions. He respected Boots' character and during the second week of training he chose Boots as one of the platoon's squad leaders.

As a squad leader Boots was in charge of a dozen men in the platoon. He was required to look after those men, help them, and be held responsible for them. Boots was very excited to become a squad leader and wrote about his new position to his mother:

> The second week I was here I was selected as a squad leader and placed in charge of twelve men. . . . I am solely responsible for those twelve men as to their drilling, behavior, attitude, and the way they keep our end of the barracks. My men have to obey me as if I were an officer, and all of them are a lot older than me. I also march at the head of the platoon, and have to execute every movement the drill sergeant calls out. All the 59 other men have to do is follow me.[13]

During training Boots and the Marines with him practiced fighting a pretend enemy. In one practice battle

General Emile Moses

Boots' platoon and several others were assigned the job of driving a pretend enemy off of a small piece of land surrounded on three sides by water. Boots took the men of his squad and secretly waded through the water to surprise the enemy forces on the land. The trick worked, and Boots and his men captured some of the enemy's positions. General Emile Moses was watching the battle and was very pleased with how Boots led his squad to victory.

Working together in a pretend battle was an exciting time for the young Marines. Every day of their training was preparing them more and more for the time when they would be sent to fight real battles with real enemies.

Though training was sometimes fun, Boots knew that real battles weren't fun. They were dangerous and very deadly. Boots didn't like to think about dying in a battle and leaving his mother and little brother and sister all alone, but he knew that he needed to think about it because it might happen. If he did die, he didn't want his mother to be left without anyone to support her, so he purchased some life insurance through the Marine Corps. With his insurance policy, if he died in the war, the United States government would pay his mother $10,000.

CHAPTER ELEVEN

A Great Surprise

Mrs. Thomas thought about her son every day while he was training at Parris Island. She couldn't visit him but she could write him letters and send him packages. Boots loved receiving packages from home. His favorite ones were the boxes that contained candy or cookies his mother had made.

Whenever Boots received a package, it didn't take the other boys in his squad long to find out if there were any sweets in it. Boots always shared the cookies and candy with his men and wrote his mother to thank her for the package and to let her know how much they all enjoyed it. He wrote her one day:

> I got the cookies and candy, and they sure were good. The cookies were a little broken up but they were still good. They sure didn't last long when my squad found out I had them.[14]

In July Boots and his platoon were sent to the rifle range to learn how to handle and shoot their rifles. Rifle training was long and difficult but was important for the Marines to learn. After finishing their training at the range, Boots and his platoon were assigned to work in the mess hall for a week. They worked eighteen hours a day on kitchen duty. During that week Boots didn't have any time to write home, and his mother began to worry about him. She wrote him a letter to ask if he was sick. When Boots' week in the mess hall ended, he wrote his mother back:

> Dear Mother,
>   I guess you think I've forgotten you all, but I haven't. I thought when I got back from the rifle range that I would have plenty of time to write but I was mistaken. The same afternoon we got back we went straight into the mess-hall on K.P. duty. . . .
>   As for you thinking I may not be well, you can forget that, because I've never felt better in my life, and have never been more satisfied. Well, in one week, I will be a full-fledged Marine, and will I be happy!

Boots ended his letter to his mother with a mysterious note: "I may have some good news for you before I leave, but I'm not sure now, so I can't say."[15]

During his time of training at Parris Island his drill instructor and other officers had noticed Boots' willingness to learn and his responsible character. They recommended him to their superiors as a young recruit who would make a good drill instructor.

Boots was excited when he learned that he might become a drill instructor. It was an important position and Boots was honored to be recommended for it, but he didn't know yet whether he would be accepted, so he decided to keep it a surprise for his mother. Being a drill instructor would mean that he wouldn't be sent into battle for a long time, but Boots didn't mind too much because he knew that his position as an instructor would be an important job that would help train more Marines and prepare them for battling against the Japanese.

Finally, in the beginning of August, 1942, Boots was accepted as a drill instructor. He excitedly wrote his mother to tell her about his new job:

Dear Mother,

Well, now you know what I meant when I said I may have a surprise for you all later. I had been told that I may be kept here as a drill instructor, but I didn't want to tell you until I was certain. One thing is certain (to my sorrow). I won't see action for a while, anyway. I do not feel so terribly bad about it, though, because I have been assigned to one of the toughest, responsible and important jobs in the Marine Corps.

Corporal Teelin (my associate) and I have to take 72 new recruits every four weeks and turn them into tough Marines who know something. Therefore you can see what I have had to learn since I've been here. I have had to learn the whole drill manual, know backwards and forwards the routine of training,

New recruits at Parris Island

USMC

and be careful of my actions at all times, to set good examples for the recruits. I have really changed. I am really tough now! Every recruit on this island has to address me as "Sir," and has to stand at attention when speaking to me. If you could see the way that I yell at the recruits when they are drilling, you would never recognize your son![16]

Becoming a drill instructor meant that Boots was responsible for training new Marines and making sure that they learned everything they needed to know before they were shipped off to the war. The responsibility of training his men for combat weighed heavily on young Boots, and he wrote his mother:

> I doubt if you will ever be able to understand the important job that I am doing. I am actually master over a recruit's way of living for four weeks and my word is absolutely law. I am actually deciding in a great way whether they will be able to survive combat or not because I am teaching them how to defend themselves. Therefore you can see that I've accepted the greatest responsibility that I have ever had or may ever hope to have.[17]

Even though he was younger than most of the men he was training, Boots took his new role seriously. He knew that his position as instructor required soberness and maturity. His job was to train the recruits under him with excellence, preparing them for whatever their future might be. His job wasn't to tell the men to learn something but instead to teach them how to learn and to show them how to act by following his own example. As he began his new job he worked his very best to follow the Marine guidelines written by Major General John Lejeune in 1921:

> The relation between officer and enlisted men should in no sense be that of superior to inferior nor that of master and servant, but rather . . . should partake of the relationship between father and son, to the extent that officers, especially commanding officers, are responsible for the physical, mental and moral welfare, as well as the discipline and military training of the young men under their command.[18]

The new platoon that Boots was training was a group of 72 men. Just like his drill instructor had done with him, Boots taught the men how to march, how to handle their rifles, and everything else a Marine recruit needed to learn.

The first group of Marines that Boots trained soon finished their time on Parris Island and prepared to ship out elsewhere. Boots was proud to see how his training had changed the 72 men under him. A few weeks ago they had entered Parris Island without knowing anything about being a Marine, but now they were leaving and were prepared to play their part in fighting the enemies that were threatening America.

While Boots was training Marines at Parris Island, Jim Sledge was also getting ready to join the war. After he graduated from high school he joined the Army Air Corps and began basic training at Miami Beach, Florida.

Lieutenant Jim Sledge

CHAPTER TWELVE

Waiting for Combat

On the 14th of October, 1942, the first platoon trained by Boots left Parris Island and he was assigned to a new batch of recruits on the next day. The most difficult part of training the men was the first few weeks when they had so much new material to learn. Boots didn't have any time to write home during those first few weeks, but afterward he wrote to his mother to let her know how he was doing:

Dear Mother,
I got your letter this morning and received the candy a couple of days ago. The candy was *very* good and *everybody* enjoyed it. . . .
Well, I guess the hardest part of my work with my new platoon is over. They are gradually losing their civilian's tendencies and becoming Marines. It makes you feel good to see them snapping around like seasoned Marines and know that you are responsible for everything they know.[19]

After he finished training his second set of men Boots received permission to go home for a few days to visit his family. He wasn't able to stay long, but he was delighted to see his family again and spend a little time catching up on everything that had happened since he had joined the Marines.

Boots returned to Parris Island the beginning of December and began working with another group of new

Left to right
Jean, Boots, Mrs. Thomas, and Jack

recruits. Sadly he would have to stay on the island and train his men over Christmas. Since he wouldn't be home for the holiday, Boots' family mailed him his presents, but told him not to open them until Christmas. Boots was glad to receive the packages, but he was so excited to find out what was in them that he wasn't sure he could wait until Christmas. He wrote his mother: "I got the three boxes you sent and have put them away in my locker, and I will now see if I have the will power to keep them there."[20]

Boots spent Christmas training his platoon on the rifle range. It was a cold, snowy Christmas for Boots and his men. Everybody was sad at being away from home and their families, but Boots was happy that he could finally open the gifts from his family. He wrote his mother: "It's really been cold up here with a little snow thrown in. . . . The box you'all sent was really nice. All in all I had a pretty nice Christmas, but of course it couldn't come up to being home."[21]

Throughout the spring and summer of 1943 Boots continued his job at Parris Island, training recruits and shipping them out to join the war in the Pacific. His continued hard work and diligence again brought him to the attention of his superiors. Because he was colorblind he wasn't allowed to be an officer, but during his time as drill instructor he was quickly promoted to corporal, then sergeant, and finally platoon sergeant.

Even though he enjoyed his work as a drill instructor and knew that it was helping the war effort, Boots still wanted to go into combat and join the battle against the Japanese. He therefore requested permission to leave Parris Island for combat in the Pacific. He didn't know whether his superior officers would let him leave Parris Island, but he hoped they would.

CHAPTER THIRTEEN

Ready for War

As the year 1943 neared its end, the Marine Corps Headquarters in Washington, D.C., announced a new addition to their forces. The war in the Pacific against the Japanese was costing America much time and many men, and the Marine Corps realized that they would need thousands of new Marines before they could hope to win the war. Nearly four hundred thousand Marines were already fighting or were already headed for the Pacific, but even more men than this would be needed. Therefore on November 11, 1943, the Marine Corps created the Fifth Marine Division, a group that would include 20,000 more Marines. The Marine Corps planned to use this new Division to attack one of the heavily-defended Japanese islands in the Pacific.

The Fifth Marine Division was nicknamed the *Spearhead* and would include new Marine recruits who had never yet been in battle. It would also include some veteran fighters who had already experienced fighting against the Japanese. The Marine Corps hoped that the veteran Marines in the Division would help the new recruits during training to learn how to better prepare themselves for fighting against the Japanese.

In early October of 1943 Boots' request for combat duty was finally granted, and with joy the young Marine saw his name included on the combat list. He was glad that his time as a drill instructor had ended and that before long he would find himself attached to a platoon preparing for immediate combat in the Pacific.

Excitedly Boots told his mother the news and then prepared to leave Parris Island for good. In just a few weeks he and other officers going into combat would be sent to Camp Lejeune in North Carolina where they would begin a nine-week course in advanced weaponry training before they were assigned to the ranks of the Spearhead, the new Fifth Marine Division.

Boots was excited about his new assignment, but he also knew that it would be a very dangerous job. The men of the Fifth Marine Division were being prepared to attack a special target area in the Pacific. Nobody knew yet where they would be sent to attack, but they did know that it would be a difficult and a risky job. Many of the Marines would die while fighting the Japanese.

While he got ready to leave Parris Island, Boots wondered: "Will I die in the battle?" He was a platoon sergeant and would therefore be helping to lead a group of men, and he knew that it was very possible that he would die because of this. Because officers led their men, this meant that they would be fighting in front of their men. Usually the men in the front died when the Japanese attacked. Boots took his role as officer seriously and accepted the leadership and self-sacrifice it required. He knew it was a dangerous job, but he knew it was what he had to do. General Holland Smith, another Marine in World War Two, explained what a leader's role in war was:

> In order for a leader to enjoy the loyalty of his sub-ordinates, he must in turn be loyal to them. . . . Our Marines expect to be led. They expect their officers to share their hardships and their hazards and I say to you solemnly that you must never, under any circumstances, expect or call upon your men to show greater spirit or courage than that which you manifest yourself.[22]

Being an officer required courage and responsibility, and also meant that a person needed to be prepared to die. Boots didn't want to die, but he knew that he might, so he started getting things ready. When he received his paycheck he sent most of the money home to his mother. While he was away at the war, the Marine Corps would continue sending money to her.

On December 9, 1943, Boots left Parris Island for the last time and traveled to Camp Lejeune, which was a base used to train Marines in *amphibious operations.*

Amphibious operations are exercises in which men on ships or boats land and attempt to take control of an enemy position on shore. The long stretches of beach at Camp Lejeune were used to prepare Marines for the landing exercises they would engage in on the islands in the Pacific against the Japanese. The Camp also had expert training facilities designed to train the men in the specific parts they would play in taking the islands from the Japanese.

When Boots arrived at Camp Lejeune he found a foot of snow on the ground. The North Carolina winter had already begun, and Boots learned with a sigh of relief that the first few weeks of his training would take place indoors. He and the Marines with him began their new training with 16-hour days of classroom instruction.

After nine weeks of indoor instruction had been completed, Boots and the other Marines at Camp Lejeune moved on to rigorous outdoor training. In a letter home Boots wrote to his mother, "I'm still working hard, and it's getting tougher every day. We moved from the nice warm barracks into tents yesterday, so you can imagine the time we are having."[23]

The outdoor training Boots and the officers with him practiced included maneuvers or exercises consisting of endurance training and pretend battles with the "enemy." Boots described one of these maneuvers to his mother in a letter home:

first case of seasickness here!

Simulated Invasion
Hospital Corpsmen Accompany Leathernecks

Boots sent pictures of his training to Jim

February 16, 1944
Dear Mother,

I received your letter this afternoon and will answer it now while I can. The training is getting more intensive as the weeks go by, and as we are supposed to finish up in about two weeks, we are going practically 24 hours a day. We got in at 2:00 A.M. yesterday morning after a ten mile hike and swimming an ice-filled river with full equipment (with dynamite exploding all around us)—and then had to get up at 5:00 o'clock![24]

Mrs. Thomas could see that her son was working very hard during his training. She knew that he was enjoying it, but she also knew that he was missing home and the family as well, so she decided to send him a box of candy and cookies to cheer him up.

Boots received the box in between his amphibious maneuvers and wrote happily to his mother:

We just got back from six days of amphibious landing maneuvers, and we got no mail or could send any while we were out there. I got the candy just before we left, and the box when I got back. Thanks a lot. You really don't know how I appreciate it, especially with the living conditions the way they are here.[25]

A week later Boots wrote another letter to his mother to describe the next maneuver he would be engaging in:

February 21, 1944
Dear Mother,

We are in the last phase of our training here, and this week is mainly an endurance test to see how much we can stand. We march 35 miles tomorrow with full equipment, and soon as we reach our objective we begin, without rest, a sustained night and day attack on the enemy, which will continue throughout the week (with us sleeping whenever and wherever we can!). We are going to be on emergency, concentrated rations the entire week, so I imagine we will be pretty hungry when we get in! I guess you can tell though from this letter that this training is agreeing with me, and the more I get, the more I know that the Japs we hit won't stand a chance! . . .

Well I've got to stop now because it's getting late and I have to "square away" my gear for tomorrow. Write so I'll have some mail when I get back.

Love to all,

Boots[26]

In their future combat missions Boots and his fellow Marines would be landing on and attacking Japanese-held islands in the Pacific. They would be transported to these islands by ships, but would need to know how to disembark from these ships onto smaller boats or landing vessels that would carry them to shore. Much of their training at Camp Lejeune focused on learning the details of these maneuvers. Moving from a large transport ship into a smaller vessel for landing was a dangerous exercise involving quick thinking and hard work. Cargo nets were hung over the ship's side, and down these the Marines climbed to board their waiting landing vessels. The landing vessels were little boats called LVT's. The LVT's were also equipped with tracks (like a tank) and were able to be driven onto beaches as well as being used as a boat.

After climbing down cargo nets into LVT's, the Marines were then transported to a North Carolina stretch of beach similar to the Japanese-held islands of the Pacific. Here their landing craft would push in as close to shore as possible.

When their landing craft reached the shore, the Marines aboard would leap out and begin battling "the enemy" while

Another View of the Mockup

from experience, this is not easy!

"From experience, this is not easy!" Boots wrote to Jim

they landed and attempted to take control of the beach and surrounding area. This maneuver was called *establishing a beachhead.*

For weeks Boots practiced this intensive training. At the end of his months of training he graduated near the head of his class. He had completed all the exercises with skill, though he told his mother: "I got a little seasick when we were coming into the beach for a landing, but it was exceptionally rough, and nearly everybody got a little sick!"[27]

The training class at New River graduated the 4th of March, 1944. Within a week Platoon Sergeant Boots Thomas boarded a troop train on his way to Camp Pendleton, California to join the rest of the Fifth Marine Division.

CHAPTER FOURTEEN

A Family of Marines

Camp Pendleton was a 200-square-mile training base for the Marine Corps. In March of 1944 the men of the Fifth Marine Division gathered at the base to complete their final training before sailing across the Pacific to join the war against Japan.

The Fifth Marine Division was a group of about 20,000 men. The men were divided into regiments and battalions. Each regiment and battalion had its own number to keep it separate from the other groups. Boots belonged to the 2nd Battalion of the 28th Regiment.

Every battalion was also divided into companies. Boots' company was called Company "E" or *Easy Company*. The commanding officer of Easy Company was Captain Dave Severance. Boots liked Captain Severance immediately when he met him. The captain was a quiet man in his mid-twenties and was well-liked by all his men.

Under Captain Severance Easy Company was divided into three platoons. Boots was the second-in-command of the third platoon. A man from Texas, Lieutenant John Wells, was in charge of the platoon. While at Camp Pendleton he and Boots would train the men of their platoon one final time before shipping out for the Pacific.

After Boots arrived at the Marine base in California he met the men of his platoon. They were a group of forty-six Marines. Boots had spent a year and a half training Marines

USMC

Training at Camp Pendleton

to send into combat. Now he was assigned one final group of Marines to train. But this time he wouldn't send them off into battle. Instead he would lead them into battle himself.

Many of the Marines in Boots' platoon had already fought the Japanese in previous battles in the Pacific. When these men saw young Boots and learned that he was their new platoon sergeant, they wondered whether Boots was wise enough to lead them into battle. Even though Boots had been trained, he hadn't ever seen a real battle before, and many of his men wondered whether he would lead them well.

Corporal Richard Wheeler was one of the men in Boots' platoon. When he first met Boots he was surprised to find someone so young and inexperienced assigned to lead the platoon. But he and the other men under Boots soon realized that they didn't need to worry about their new leader. Corporal Wheeler later wrote about Boots, "He had been a Marine for only a short time but his quick mind and his aptitude for leadership had enabled him to advance rapidly."[28]

As the men began to get to know Sergeant Boots, they grew to like and respect him even though he was so young. Before long they nicknamed him "Thomas the Tiger." Corporal Wheeler explained why:

> The company's platoon sergeants included blond, curly-headed Ernest I. "Boots" Thomas, who was something of a phenomenon. . . . He was ordinarily soft-spoken, but when he issued orders on the drillfield he deepened his voice until it resembled a low growl. He was liked and admired by the men, who referred to him as "Thomas the Tiger."[29]

The men under Boots weren't the only ones surprised at him. Even Captain Severance wondered about Sergeant Boots: How would he handle himself in battle? "I was concerned about the platoon sergeant's lack of combat experience," Captain Severance wrote.[30]

But, after the men's training at Camp Pendleton began, Captain Severance no longer had any doubts about Boots. He wrote: "Any apprehension I may have had about his ability to command respect in this atmosphere was soon discounted when I observed his leadership qualities and maturity."[31] As Captain Severance watched how Boots handled and led his men, the captain realized that he didn't need to worry anymore. He could see that Boots would perform his job well no matter what might happen.

The men in Boots' platoon had come from every corner of the United States. One of them, Sergeant Henry Hansen, was in his mid-twenties and had said goodbye to his

Sergeant Henry "Hank" Hansen

Corporal Charles "Chuck" Lindberg

home in Somerville, Massachusetts to join the Marines when the war started. He was a Marine paratrooper and had already fought the Japanese on other islands in the Pacific. He was nicknamed "Hank" and was given the role of Platoon Guide.

Donald Ruhl was another member of Boots' platoon. He was a private from Joliet, Montana. Ruhl liked being a Marine, but he didn't like the training. He thought it was boring and repetitive to spend day after day practicing an attack. Ruhl couldn't wait until he could actually board a ship and sail across the Pacific to go meet the Japanese in battle.

Another member of the platoon was Corporal Charles "Chuck" Lindberg, one of the platoon's flamethrowers. He was a native of North Dakota and was one of ten children. Chuck had enlisted in the Marine Corps a month after Pearl Harbor. Then he volunteered for the Marine Raiders and fought the Japanese on the islands of Guadalcanal and Bougainville. He was an experienced Marine and was regarded with awe by the younger members of the platoon.

Thrown together from all parts of the country into the Marine base in California, the forty-six men in Boots' platoon started out as strangers to each other. But, as they worked together during their training, they gradually changed from a group of individuals into a close-knit body of Marines. Each member of the group knew how important it was to learn to work together as a unit. They understood that when they entered battle against the Japanese they would need to know how to trust their leaders and how to rely on and help each other. This knowledge would often mean the difference between life and death for the men.

During their long days of training the platoon formed itself into a sort of family. The men learned to watch out for each other and to help with difficult jobs even when they didn't want to. Teamwork and thinking about others was going to be a big part of their task when they finally met the Japanese.

Training at Camp Pendleton wasn't easy. Just like at Camp Lejeune in North Carolina, the Marines practiced attacking and battling with the enemy. With bombs exploding and mortars crashing around them, Boots and his men practiced crawling across ground strung with barbed-wire to attack enemy fortifications in front of them. They learned how to enter and search caves where enemy soldiers were hiding and how to attack and capture pillboxes, which were small forts made out of concrete. The Japanese used these to conceal their machine guns and attack the Marines as they moved forward. Sometimes the pillboxes were buried underground with only a few feet of the walls visible from the surface.

Throughout this training the Marines practiced many maneuvers similar to what Boots had already learned during his specialized training at Camp Lejeune. Sergeant Boots, with Lieutenant Wells, led his men in disembarking from ships into smaller landing craft which ferried the men to shore, where they scrambled onto "enemy" beaches ready to battle the Japanese.

The men of Boots' platoon quickly learned that leaving their ships was a dangerous job. While they climbed down cargo nets to board their smaller landing vessels, they had to be careful not to get crushed. Because they were on the ocean, their ships and boats were lifted by the waves and often crashed into each other, endangering the lives of the men who were scaling their sides. With these and other dangers threatening the Marines, their officers worked diligently to be sure that their men received as much training and protection as possible.

Dealing with ships smashing into the waves and each other wasn't the only worry that the Marines had. Once they reached shore, their landing craft often had to stop before it reached the beach because of debris or other things blocking its path. This forced the men to leave their boats, jump into the water, and wade ashore. Sometimes their gear got washed away in the waves. Other times the waves tipped their boats and the Marines had to try to swim to shore after their

USMC

boats sank. Every step of their training was dangerous and the Marines quickly learned that they would need to work together to stay alive.

After they landed on shore, the Marines knew that they wouldn't be alone while they were fighting the enemy. Tanks would also come ashore to assist them, and mortar and machine gun crews would work alongside them while they battled to capture the island from the Japanese.

The intensive training continued through the summer months, and as the days of August passed Boots knew that he and his men would be leaving the States soon. At last, in September of 1944 they received orders to board ships and prepare to go to sea.

CHAPTER FIFTEEN

Island X

Finally, after months of training, the men of the Fifth Marine Division crammed themselves into trucks and buses and traveled thirty-five miles south to San Diego where they boarded transport ships waiting for them in the California harbor. From there they began a week-long voyage to Port Hilo on the Big Island of Hawaii.

Disembarking at Hilo, the Marines were transported by truck and rail to Camp Tarawa, a forty-thousand-acre camp nestled in the volcanic mountains of Hawaii. Here the Division would complete its training and await orders for shipping out into combat.

Arriving on the island in mid-September, Boots wrote home after he had settled in to his new surroundings. Because of military security he wasn't allowed to tell his mother that he was on Hawaii, but he knew that if he described his camp she would be able to guess where he was:

Dear Mother,

You've probably gotten a card by now with my address and letting you know I arrived O.K. If not, this will serve the purpose. We had a pretty good trip over, but it felt mighty good to set foot on solid ground.

We're on a beautiful island with our camp situated practically in the clouds. So we have nice warm weather during the day, and use three blankets at night. All in all I'm not a bit displeased with my new "home."

USMC

Raising the flag at Camp Tarawa

Later I'll write you more about it—that is, as much as censorship permits![32]

During their months of training none of the Marines knew where they were headed. They understood that they would be attacking the Japanese on one of their Pacific islands, but nobody knew which island it would be. The military authorities didn't tell anyone because they didn't want the Japanese to find out where the Marines were headed. Instead they simply called the island "Island X."

But, now that they were in Hawaii, the top secret information that everyone had been waiting for finally arrived. The Marines weren't told yet, but during the third week of October the division staff and the regimental commanders of the Fifth Division received word that they would be engaging in an assault on the island of Iwo Jima.

Iwo Jima was a little island located southeast of the mainland of Japan. It was almost unknown to the outside world, but the name of this tiny speck in the Pacific Ocean would soon become a household word throughout America and around the globe. It was located at the southern tip of the Nanpo Shoto, a chain of islands stretching southward from Japan. Iwo Jima meant *Sulphur Island,* and was a small land mass of less than eight square miles.

Iwo Jima

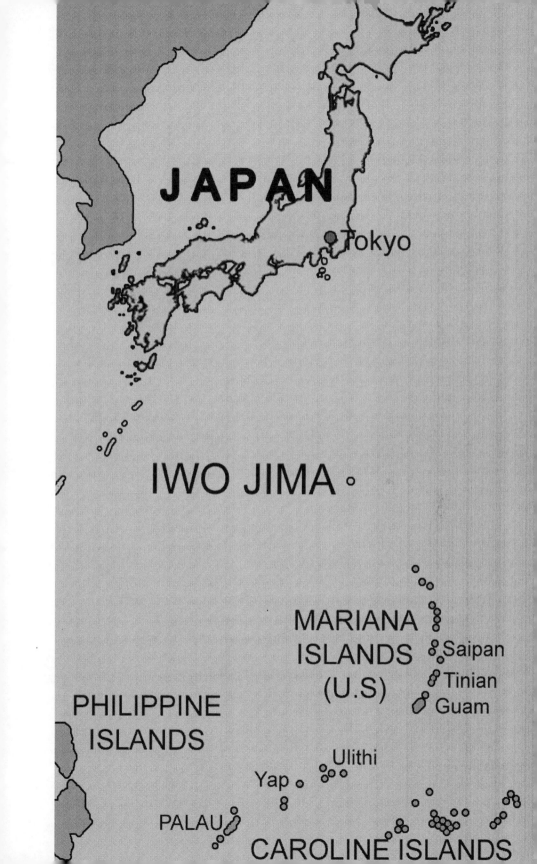

Even though it was small, the little island was of great strategic importance to both America and Japan. Iwo Jima lay directly in the flight path taken by American B-29 bombers as they flew to Japan on their bombing missions. The Japanese had built a radio base on Iwo Jima, and its radar was able to pick up the sound of the U.S. bombers long before they reached their targets. Whenever they heard the bombers approaching, radiomen on Iwo Jima sent immediate word to Tokyo to alert them of the coming air raids. This meant that gunners in Tokyo were ready to shoot down the American bombers as soon as they flew in over Japan.

The Japanese had also constructed two airfields on little Iwo Jima. From these fields Japanese fighter planes (known as Zeros) launched attacks on nearby American-held locations. They also attacked and shot down the U.S. bombers as they passed over. Because the bombers were larger and heavier planes, they were easy targets for the Japanese fighter planes, especially if the American bombers were damaged during their bombing runs on Japan.

Another problem that faced the American bombers was that their planes often ran low on fuel. When they bombed Japan they had to take off from a group of islands 700 miles away and often didn't have enough fuel left for the return trip. This meant that many planes were lost at sea because they couldn't make it back to an American base. If the Americans had control of Iwo Jima, they would have a much shorter distance to fly and could land on that island if they needed to refuel. This would save the lives of thousands of American bomb crews.

Iwo Jima was also very special to the Japanese. It was only 650 miles south of Tokyo, the capital of Japan, and was regarded by the Japanese as the entrance to mainland Japan and the gateway to the Japanese homeland. The military commanders in America hoped that if they took possession of the island it would help to show Japan that they couldn't win the war against the United States and that they should stop

USMC

B-29 Bomber

fighting.

Now that the regimental commanders knew where their men would be fighting, they geared the training for each of the regiments to focus on the specific part it would play in the coming attack. Sergeant Boots Thomas and his men were part of the 28th Regiment. This regiment's assignment was an attack on Mount Suribachi, located on the southern tip of Iwo Jima. Mount Suribachi was an extinct volcano that guarded the southern beaches of the little island. It was over 550 feet tall and would be a very difficult and dangerous mountain to attack.

For the rest of their time in training in Hawaii, Boots and his men practiced attacking and capturing a large mountain. They didn't know which mountain they would be attacking when they arrived at their real battlefield, but this training would help them learn how to work together with other platoons to surround and overcome an enemy located on a large and frightening mountain.

Throughout the final weeks of 1944 their training continued and, as the year 1945 arrived, Boots and the Marines of the Fifth Division boarded transports for a final dress rehearsal prior to their sail to Iwo Jima. In a little over a month they would arrive at their final destination, where the Japanese were already waiting for them.

CHAPTER SIXTEEN

Living and Dying
for the Emperor

Over 20,000 Japanese soldiers guarded the little Pacific island known as Iwo Jima. They were commanded by Lieutenant General Tadamichi Kuribayashi, a *samurai* or member of the Japanese warrior cast. General Kuribayashi had spent six years in the United States as a young man and had learned a few things about Americans. He knew what plans and weapons the American Marines would use to attack the island, and he was determined that they would never win the battle as long as he was alive.

General Kuribayashi also knew that the Americans were determined to win. He would need all of his skill and

Japanese General Tadamichi Kuribayashi

wisdom to fight them because they would bring many more men than he had, and they would bring more weapons as well.

Iwo Jima wasn't very big, but General Kuribayashi saw that he could turn the island into a fortress if he and his men worked hard enough. The land on Iwo Jima was divided into three sections. The northern end of the island rose from the ocean in steep volcanic cliffs that opened onto a flat plateau 360 feet above the water. The island was full of volcanic activity, and the ground of this northern area was warmed by the fumes and fires of the lava buried deep beneath its surface.

At the southern end of the island was Mount Suribachi, a second volcano. Suribachi rose 556 feet above the island's beaches and was visible from sea long before the rest of the land came into view. Its massive height dominated the landscape of the little island.

Between Mount Suribachi in the south and the volcanic heights in the north lay a strip of level ground where the Japanese had built their two airstrips or runways for their fighter planes.

After examining the island, General Kuribayashi knew that the only place where the Americans could land in their coming invasion would be on the southern beaches located just north of Mount Suribachi. If that was where the Americans would land, then the Japanese defenses on the beaches needed to be strong. The Japanese general ordered large coast-defense guns, machine gun nests, mortar pits, and pillboxes to be built along the tops of the beaches. He commanded his men to hide these defensive positions in caves or conceal them with sand or debris so that the Marines wouldn't be able to find them. With these weapons ready, General Kuribayashi hoped that he could drive the Americans back into the ocean when they landed to attack.

Across the rest of the island the Japanese built more pillboxes, bunkers, blockhouses, and other gun emplacements to defend themselves against the coming Marines. They buried tanks up to their turrets so that the Americans wouldn't see

Japanese pillboxes overlooking a beach in Japan

them. General Kuribayashi also ordered his men to construct a deadly system of mine fields, trenches, and anti-tank ditches to crisscross the island.

The Japanese camouflaged all their defensive positions and buried many of them underground so that they wouldn't be destroyed when the American bombers began dropping load after load of bombs onto the island. The Japanese also built tunnels and underground passageways that connected each pillbox and bunker to the others. By using these tunnels during the battle the Japanese soldiers would be able to catch the Americans off guard by attacking them without being seen.

General Kuribayashi also ordered the men to dig tunnels and create caves deep underground where the Japanese could live in safety during the American bombardment and attack. All supplies of food, water, and ammunition were stored in these underground caves and caverns to protect them from the coming battle.

Digging tunnels and caves through Iwo Jima's volcanic rock and mountains was easy at times, but at other times it became very dangerous. Because the island was formed out of extinct volcanoes, many caverns and passageways already existed beneath the surface of the ground. The Japanese used these caverns and dug as many more as they needed. The volcanic stone was soft enough to be carved out easily, but sometimes poisonous gases came out of the rocks while the men worked. To protect themselves the Japanese had to wear gas masks.

Another danger during digging was the heat from the volcanic steam vents. In some caves the temperature rose to 160 degrees, making work very difficult. The men had to be careful in these areas and could only work for a few minutes before taking a rest. One benefit of the heat was that the Japanese didn't need stoves to cook their food. They could put a pan of rice on the ground and it would be cooked and ready to eat within 20 minutes.

When they were finished the Japanese had discovered or created over eleven miles of tunnels and underground passages. Some of the caves they used were large enough to house hundreds of men. This was where the men ate and slept. Even the hospitals were located underground, as well as radio rooms and supply rooms. The Japanese were careful to create several tunnels or exits for each of these rooms. If one of the exits was blocked off or attacked by the Americans, the soldiers could escape through one of the other tunnels.

Japanese Lieutenant Musashino Kikuzo, a young officer on Iwo Jima, wrote proudly of his personal defense area:

USMC

Japanese machine gun bunker

Japanese tank

My air-raid shelter had been strongly constructed. There were eleven entrances to it. The shelter had been linked with defense positions, and they were well camouflaged. I was proud of my shelter and positions, saying that they were the strongest on Iwo Jima.[33]

General Kuribayashi ordered special preparations for Mount Suribachi. It was a very important position to hold because of its height. From its top the Japanese would be able to watch the battle over the rest of the island and could see everything that the Marines were doing. This would give the Japanese the ability to attack the Americans where they were the weakest and to direct their artillery fire with deadly accuracy against the Marines. General Kuribayashi wanted Mount Suribachi protected and defended at all costs.

The Japanese worked diligently to prepare special defenses for the mountain. They hollowed out tunnels and caves inside Suribachi to hide their troops and weapons. On the mountain's tall slopes they built artillery, rocket, and mortar pits. Blockhouses made out of concrete were constructed at its base and sides, and pillboxes were built and filled with all types of weapons from automatic rifles to artillery and coast-defense guns. Antiaircraft guns, rocket launchers, and stationary tanks were carefully placed and so well camouflaged that they were almost invisible. The Japanese also stockpiled rifles, machine guns, and hand grenades inside the mountain.

USMC

**View from inside a Japanese defense position
overlooking the landing beaches and airfield**

General Kuribayashi established his headquarters at the north end of the island. From there he directed his men while they prepared for the American attack. While they worked General Kuribayashi reminded his soldiers that they were serving the emperor of Japan. The emperor required that all of his men must be prepared to fight and die for him and for Japan. The Japanese knew that they were commanded to fight until they died. They weren't allowed to surrender, even if the Americans won.

In their country the Japanese were taught that their emperor was a god and that he must be obeyed like a god. The emperor commanded all Japanese to give him something called *unquestioning obedience.* This meant that the Japanese must obey the emperor and fight for him and die for him without asking whether they were fighting for something good or not. Even if their emperor asked them to do something wrong, the Japanese were required to obey him.

While they worked on their caves and defenses on Iwo Jima, the Japanese soldiers thought about this and decided that they would fight until they died. If they couldn't win the battle against the Americans, they decided that they would kill themselves instead of being captured. They would do this for their emperor because it was what he commanded them. The Japanese didn't realize that this was wrong.

CHAPTER SEVENTEEN

Somewhere in the Pacific

More than twenty thousand Japanese defenders guarded the few square miles of rock and sand rising from the ocean floor that formed the tiny island of Iwo Jima. During the summer and fall of 1944 these defenders began receiving the first tastes of the coming invasion as the skies over the island were darkened with countless formations of American bombers. Beginning mid-June and continuing into February of 1945, tons of bombs and explosives were dropped on the little island in an attempt to destroy the fortifications that the Japanese had constructed.

Unfortunately, the intense bombing didn't do much damage to General Kuribayashi's defenses. American planes photographed the island before and after the bombing and noted that the Japanese continued to improve their fortifications despite the falling bombs.

The American photographic planes continued to find and record the defense positions on the little island. By February of 1945 they had identified over six hundred Japanese pillboxes, blockhouses, caves, and other defensive structures. What the Americans didn't realize was that there were hundreds of defensive positions that they still hadn't discovered.

In early 1945 Boots and the other men of the Fifth Marine Division finished their final training maneuvers in Hawaii and boarded their waiting transport ships to head to Iwo Jima. The Marines of the Fifth Marine Division now became

US Bomber flies over Mount Suribachi

part of the Fifth Amphibious Corps, which was composed of three complete divisions—the Third, Fourth, and Fifth. This Corps had a combined total of over 70,000 Marines. It was commanded by Major General Harry Schmidt and Lieutenant General Holland Smith. The fleet accompanying them, under command of Vice Admiral Kelly Turner, totaled 485 ships, over seventy of which were transport ships housing the men and their supplies.

The amount of supplies needed for 70,000 men was enormous. Besides food, the Marines also needed ammunition for their weapons and gasoline for their vehicles.

The medical personnel needed bandages, medicines, and surgical instruments for the countless wounded they would be treating. The men had to bring all their own water since the island didn't have any natural water source. One other thing in the list of supplies that the men might not have noticed was the thousands of wooden crosses ready to be erected over the graves that would be dug for the dead.

While they were aboard ship on their way to Iwo Jima, the Marines finally learned the location of where they were going. Captain Dave Severance explained to Lieutenant Wells and Sergeant Boots the part they and their men would be playing in attacking and capturing Mount Suribachi. Boots looked in awe at the map of Iwo Jima spread before them and wondered how they would capture the mountain. Captain Severance also wondered how it could be done. He knew the men would do their best, but he was afraid that they might all die in the attempt.

The Marines were told that they would be landing on the southern beaches. The military authorities didn't know how strong General Kuribayashi's defenses were, but they did know that it would probably take a great deal of fighting to be able to capture just the beaches themselves. In an interview with newspapermen and radiomen to explain what would happen once they landed on Iwo Jima, Admiral Turner explained that the battle for the little island would be very difficult and that many men were expected to die:

> The defenses are thick. The number of defenders there is considerable and well suited to the size of the island. It is, I believe, as well defended a fixed position, particularly an island position, as exists in the world today.
>
> We expect losses. We expect losses of ships and we expect losses of troops, and we believe they will be considerable. We are taking steps, as far as our knowledge and skill and intent is concerned, to reduce

General Holland Smith

these losses as far as we can, to as low figures as we can. But, we are going to have losses.[34]

General Holland Smith also spent time thinking about how many men would die when the battle began. The thought that so many of his Marines would die saddened him, but he knew that they needed to capture the island to win the war.

The weight of knowing that so many men would die was a heavy burden, but General Smith found comfort in reading the Scriptures and knowing that attacking the island was what needed to be done. He wrote:

I was not afraid of the outcome of the battle. I knew we would win. We always did. But contemplation of the cost in lives caused me many sleepless nights. My only source of comfort was in reading of the tribulations of leaders described in the Bible. Never before had I realized the spiritual uplift and solace a man on the eve of a great trial receives from the pages of that book.[35]

While 70,000 Marines sailed across the Pacific Ocean toward Iwo Jima, many of the men thought about the battle that was coming and prayed with David: "My times are in Your hand; deliver me from the hand of my enemies" (Psa. 31:15).

CHAPTER EIGHTEEN

Battle for Iwo Jima

February 19, 1945 dawned beautifully. The massive American fleet had arrived off the coast of Iwo Jima and now, as the sun began to rise, the thousands of Marines aboard the ships lined the rails and looked toward shore to catch their first glimpse of the little island they would be attacking. A small dark shore met their eyes, with an imposing Mount Suribachi towering hundreds of feet above them to their left.

The day of battle had finally arrived. The Marines were awakened by 3:00 A.M. A special breakfast was served this morning: steak and eggs. After it had been devoured, the men began loading into their landing vessels in preparation for their transport to shore. Soon the little LVT's were bobbing up and down in the water alongside the larger transport ships while they waited for the order to head toward the beaches. The first wave of troops was scheduled to reach the shore at 9:00 A.M.

Boots' group, the third platoon of Easy Company, had been divided into two LVT's. Lieutenant Wells took one LVT with half the men and Sergeant Thomas led the second with the remainder of the platoon. As the morning moments slipped by the young Marines within the small LVT's groaned as the little boats rose and fell on the ocean's swells. The thought of the upcoming battle sobered them, but perhaps more feared at the moment was the dreaded threat of seasickness.

At a few minutes past 6:30 A.M. the pre-landing bombardment began. The battleships and cruisers of the fleet opened fire and pounded their pre-assigned targets. Red bursts exploded onshore, marking the missiles' impacts in the early morning light as tons of shells burst against the Japanese defenses. The Marines in their landing crafts watched the deafening bombardment as shell after shell launched from the ships, raising earsplitting explosions as they met the land. With hundreds of rounds shaking the island from end to end in the mighty barrage, little Iwo was soon almost invisible in a cloud of dust and smoke.

USMC

Pre-landing bombardment

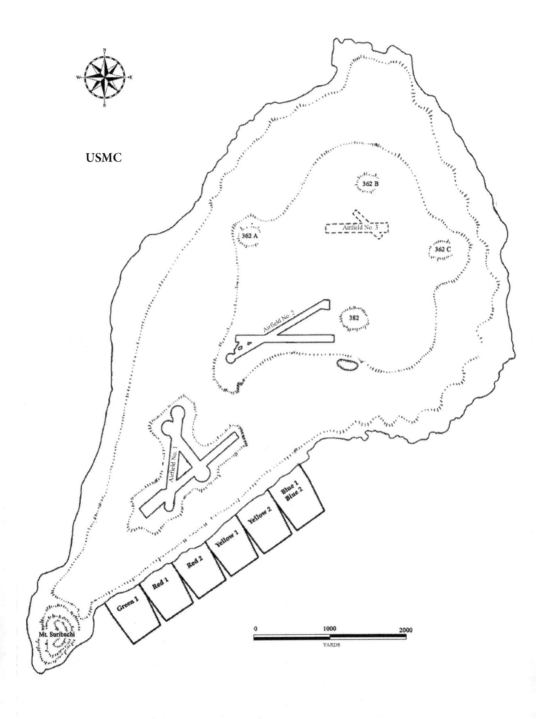

Map of Iwo Jima landing beaches

The bombardment continued until 8:00, when the firing ceased. A deadly silence filled the fleet while the world itself appeared to pause to catch its breath. Then, suddenly, overhead the roar of 120 engines was heard as carrier planes approached the island, flying in to drop their final bombs before the landing force took over.

At 8:25 the ships again opened fire, this time aiming every shell at the Japanese defenses on the beaches. The sands would soon be filled with their own men, and this was the Navy's final chance to knock out the remaining defense positions along the shore. As thousands upon thousands of shells rained down on the beaches, the Marines in their waiting boats watched, wondering what would be left after the bombardment had ceased. Was it possible that the enemy could have survived after all that bombing?

While the Marines wondered, the Japanese simply burrowed deeper into their caves and tunnels and patiently waited for the bombardment to end.

At 8:30 the signal to proceed to land was given, and in formation the LVT's churned toward the island. As if on parade, their ranks were divided into waves, with 250 to 300 yards between each line.

Iwo Jima's south beach stretched from the base of Suribachi toward the northern end of the island. It had been divided by the military commanders into five-hundred-yard sections, and each section was assigned a color. The 5th Division was to land on beaches Green and Red, while the 4th Division was given beaches Yellow and Blue. Boots' platoon and the other men of the 28th Marines were assigned to Green Beach, the southernmost beach which lay directly under the eyes of the volcano. Their assignment was to cut straight across the island to the west coast in an attempt to separate Suribachi from the remainder of Iwo Jima. Once this was accomplished, they would then begin attacking the volcano itself.

At 9:00 A.M. the first wave of Marines hit the beaches. They had hoped that their LVT's would be able to drive across

Crossing the beaches

the shore and up the beaches before unloading their cargo of
Marines. But, as the landing crafts churned out of the water,
they sank deeply in the soft volcanic ash and found themselves
unable to climb the beaches at all. They were therefore forced
to drop their Marines at the waterline. Undaunted, the
men sprinted from their vessels and dashed across the open
beaches.

When the first Marines landed the beaches were
strangely quiet. No sign of the enemy was visible. Wave after
wave of Marines followed the first men ashore and soon the

beaches were filled with men, yet Iwo Jima remained silent.

Boots' company wasn't scheduled to land until the twelfth wave. Therefore he and his men watched the Marines in front of them to see what was happening on shore.

As Boots' platoon neared the shore and wave after wave of Marines landed, filling the beach, the Japanese also watched—and waited. Under General Kuribayashi's orders, the defenders had held their fire until the beaches were swarming with Marines. Now, as over 6,000 men filled the narrow stretch of land, the island suddenly burst into deadly action.

USMC

Marines approach shore

At a given signal little Iwo Jima erupted into devastating activity as Japanese mortars, bullets, and shells whizzed through the landing area, exploding LVT's as they crawled ashore and brutally thinning the ranks of Marines scattered along the crowded beach. The Japanese artillery, mortars, and machine gun fire swept the landing area and poured into the congested beaches. Marines scattered and ran to find cover as the enemy weapons raked every square inch of sand.

While the deadly barrage continued onshore, Boots' LVT still churned toward the beaches. Sergeant Boots climbed onto the vessel's gunwale in order to get a better look at the landing site while his men crouched low behind him, afraid of enemy snipers.

Though most of the Japanese were aiming at the Marines on the beaches, some of their guns were also firing

at the landing craft heading toward shore. The Marines of
Boots' platoon watched as an LVT near theirs received a direct
hit from the Japanese and sank instantly. Even though most
of the men were rescued, Boots' men began to wonder if they
would reach the shore alive.

Finally Boots' landing craft churned ashore and rolled
to a stop just above the level of the surf. Sergeant Boots called
to Wheeler and Louie Adrian to unload the vessel's supplies of
ammunition, food, and water, and led the rest of his men onto
the beach in front of them. As they exited the landing craft
the Japanese fire found them and one of the men was shot
in the leg. One of the platoon's corpsmen, Clifford Langley,
dressed the wound, then left the wounded man on the beach
to be evacuated to a hospital ship offshore. Meanwhile Boots
led the rest of his men through the hail of bullets and shells
toward their rendezvous area, where they would receive
further orders. Lieutenant Wells and the rest of the platoon
arrived a few minutes later and rushed to catch up with Boots
and the other men.

While machine guns and mortars fired and exploded
around them, Lieutenant Wells and Sergeant Boots led their
platoon across the beach as the men ducked low in an attempt
to keep alive. The men had almost made it across the stretch
of beach when a mortar exploded in their midst. Another one
of the platoon members was dangerously wounded and had
to be left on the beach for evacuation. The rest of the men
followed as Lieutenant Wells led them forward up a sand dune
and across a second stretch of beach.

On the other side of the beach the platoon found an
abandoned Japanese trench. Quickly the men jumped into the
trench and ducked low to avoid the machine gun fire rattling
around them.

Across the island from every direction the Japanese
fire exploded, bursting furiously on the thousands of Marines
filling the beaches and fighting their way inland. But, despite
the heavy fire, the Marines were surprised to find that they

couldn't see a single Japanese defender. General Kuribayashi's orders to conceal and camouflage all their defensive positions had been carried out so well that it was almost impossible to locate the pillboxes and mortar pits where the men were hiding. To the Marines, it seemed like they were fighting an invisible enemy.

With other platoons battling the invisible foe at their right and left, Lieutenant Wells and Sergeant Boots slowly and painfully led their platoon across the open ground and miraculously arrived at the rendezvous area with no further casualties. Captain Dave Severance and the rest of company headquarters were already there waiting for them.

Soon after the men arrived, Captain Severance gave them their next assignment. The First Battalion had crossed the island to the opposite beach on the western shore, but they needed reinforcements. He therefore sent Boots' platoon forward to help.

Fighting step by step inland, the Marines soon discovered that nothing was what it appeared to be on the little island. Countless times the Americans would kill the enemy defenders of a pillbox or bunker and move on. Then, suddenly, they would see the pillbox spring to life behind them as more Japanese entered and attacked them from behind. The Marines soon began to realize that the defenses were a maze of interconnected positions that would always spring back to life unless they were completely destroyed. Tanks and demolition crews therefore worked systematically through the lines blowing up every pillbox, blockhouse, and bunker they could find, whether they appeared occupied or not.

Lieutenant Wells and Boots led their men to the western beach without any more casualties. There they established a line of defense and noted with surprise that the

USMC

sun was already beginning to set. It had taken almost all day just to make it across the island. Now they had to form a line and hold their position through the coming night.

As darkness fell the weary Marines knew that the Japanese might take advantage of the night hours to attack the Americans in the dark. Boots and his men knew that there were thousands of Japanese hiding somewhere near. If they snuck out of their caves and tunnels, they could easily kill the few Marines huddled on the western shore.

Cold, tired, and hungry, Boots and his men sat or lay along their lines when night came, waiting for the morning. Lieutenant Wells and Boots had told the men not to move during the night. If they did, someone might mistake them for a Japanese soldier and kill them. But, just in case someone did need to move, the Americans were given a password to use so that everyone would know they were Americans.

USMC

Some of Boots' men had found a shallow ditch to spend the night in. Private Edward Kurelik, a Marine from Chicago, sat at one end of the ditch. Where he sat, the trench ran through another ditch, creating a cross. Other men from the squad huddled in two of the other trench entrances, leaving the fourth opening empty. Unable to sleep, Kurelik sat through the long night and watched the empty trench in front of him.

The Marines were afraid that the Japanese would attack during the night, but the cold hours slipped slowly by without much disturbance. At last the men could feel the dawn drawing near in the early morning. Then, suddenly, a sharp cry rang out on the still night air:

"Studebaker!"

It was Edward Kurelik who yelled. He had called out the American password because he thought he heard someone creeping toward him along the empty ditch in front of him.

Immediately after Kurelik cried out he heard an angry response in Japanese as a grenade came flying toward him. The grenade landed in the midst of the men and exploded instantly.

The startled Marines quickly jumped up and began firing their rifles into the ditch, but the Japanese soldier escaped. The squad's leader Howard Snyder threw a few grenades into the empty ditch, but the enemy was nowhere to be found.

Turning back to their comrades, the Marines found that two of their members had been wounded by the Japanese grenade. Phil Christman had been slightly wounded by shrapnel, and Ed Kurelik had received severe wounds in one leg. John Bradley, one of the platoon's corpsmen, carefully crawled toward the squad to dress the men's wounds. As he crawled he called out loudly to the men to let them know who he was so that they wouldn't think he was a Japanese soldier and shoot him.

Sergeant Boots checked on the men and then reported

the incident to Lieutenant Wells. When he heard what had happened Lieutenant Wells told the men not to use the password anymore that night. If anyone suspicious came near them, he told them to shoot without asking questions.

Boots and his men settled back into their ditches and hoped that the sun would rise soon. It had been almost a full day since they had first landed on Iwo Jima. Already many of the men were wounded. Many other men had been killed.

During the night hours commanding officers had begun taking account of the men under their command. Slowly and painfully they counted how many men were wounded and how many were dead. When their count was finished they noted sadly that already 600 men were dead and almost two thousand had been wounded. The fight for little Iwo Jima had already been a bloody battle, and they hadn't even been fighting for a full day yet.

CHAPTER NINETEEN

Attacking Mount Suribachi

When daylight finally arrived the battle began all over again. Japanese mortar and artillery shells screamed through the lines of Marines stretched across the island. New orders quickly arrived for Lieutenant Wells and Boots. They were commanded to lead their men back across the island to join the rest of the Second Battalion and prepare to attack Mount Suribachi.

Sergeant Boots led the men while Lieutenant Wells brought up the rear. Edward Kurelik was too badly wounded to walk, so the men made a stretcher out of a poncho and carried him along with them until they found an aid station where they could leave him to be evacuated to a hospital ship.

Boots led his men through trenches and ditches and any other cover he could find. Machine gun fire rattled around them and exploding mortars kept them ducking low to try to stay alive as they made their way back to Easy Company headquarters. They finally reached it about noon. Captain Severance was there commanding the men who were moving forward to attack Mount Suribachi.

The Japanese had created such good defenses around the mountain that it took the Marines all day just to break through the defenses and move up a little closer to the base of Suribachi. When it began to get dark the men again took cover for the night in shell holes that had been left by mortar explosions and bombs.

Because they were so close to the mountain the men

were in great danger of being attacked by the Japanese during the night. Lieutenant Wells and Sergeant Boots knew that their men would need extra protection that night, so Boots ran back to company headquarters and found several rolls of barbed wire. He brought these back to where his men were hiding in their shell holes. Boots planned to stretch the wire along the ground in front of his men so that the Japanese wouldn't be able to reach them during a night attack.

To stretch the wire along the open ground meant that someone would have to stand exposed while stretching out the wire. Japanese machine gunners would be able to see them doing this and could easily shoot and kill them. Lieutenant Wells and Boots knew how dangerous it would be to stretch the wire, so they decided to do it themselves. Because they were the leaders, they knew that the most dangerous job was theirs. Several men from their platoon helped them. Moving as quickly as possible, they stretched out the barbed wire and ran back to their shell holes for cover. Miraculously nobody was hurt.

After their job was finished the men ducked low in their shell holes and wondered what would happen in the morning. They would attack Mount Suribachi after sunrise. But what would happen then? Boots and Lieutenant Wells knew that the battle for the mountain would be very difficult and many men would probably die. It was hard for the two of them to think about how many of their men would be dead before the fight was over. Lieutenant Wells wrote about what he was thinking:

USMC

I was sick, sick, sick. To me it appeared that we had lost the battle before we began. Tomorrow they will expect us to attack that mighty fortress with only a handful of men. All the planning, the precautions, the mental and physical strain to see that the men would be present and properly equipped for the great battle ahead was for nothing. . . . All I could think about was the great loss of men.[36]

The attack on Suribachi was scheduled to begin at 8:25 A.M. An hour before this Sergeant Boots moved carefully from crater to crater to tell his men to get ready for the coming attack and to let them know that there would be tanks coming with them to help in the battle. The tanks would be able to destroy the Japanese defense positions that the men couldn't overcome and would protect the men from some of the Japanese artillery and fire.

Boots' men were glad to hear that tanks would be helping them. They sat in their shell holes and waited for the tanks to arrive, but the minutes slowly passed and the tanks never came. They had run out of fuel the night before and had been driven back to the beach to refuel. But travel across the island took so long that the tanks weren't able to make it back to the mountain in time for the attack.

Captain Dave Severance knew how important it was to have the tanks helping his men, so he postponed the attack and hoped that they would arrive. But, when 9:00 came and the tanks still hadn't come, Captain Severance was ordered to have his men attack without them.

Lieutenant Wells received the order to advance. He knew the tanks weren't coming and he was afraid that all of his men would die in the attack. But he knew that they had to take the mountain, so he raised his weapon and led his men forward. As he advanced Boots ran in front of him to pull away the barbed wire that they had stretched out to protect the men. Now the barbed wire was in the way as they began their attack, so Boots pulled it aside to let the men get by. While he worked he didn't realize that there were three or four Japanese pillboxes just a few yards from where he stood. The pillboxes were so well hidden that he didn't see them. But, in God's providence, he was able to move the wire and lead the men forward before the Japanese opened fire.

The Marines dashed forward toward the mountain while the Japanese fired machine guns and sent mortars screaming overhead. They hadn't gone far before the men began to fall. Raymond Strahm was the platoon's first casualty that morning as a piece of shrapnel sliced through his helmet and wounded him in the head. Robert Blevins, another one of Boots' men, dropped next, wounded in the leg.

Still the men ran on, while bullets whistled past them as

USMC

they ran. A moment later a mortar exploded, killing Corporal Edward Romero. Richard Wheeler was the next to fall when two mortars exploded beside him, seriously wounding him and killing another member of the platoon.

They had already lost many men, but Lieutenant Wells and Boots led the rest of their Marines forward toward the mountain. At last they reached the mountain's base. Many of their men had lagged behind, but Donald Ruhl and Hank Hansen were still with them. Before them a massive Japanese blockhouse stood to their right and a pillbox to their left. The two defenses were connected by a trench. Bullets and shells screamed around them, and Ruhl and Hansen thought the trench would be a good place to duck for cover. They raced up to the trench and were about to dive in when they stopped

USMC

in surprise. The trench was full of Japanese soldiers! The Japanese ran for cover while the Americans opened fire with their rifles.

While they ran one of the Japanese soldiers threw a grenade at Ruhl and Hansen. It landed between the two Marines. Ruhl saw the grenade first and knew that it would explode and kill Hansen. He cried "Look out, Hank!" and threw himself on top of the grenade. It immediately exploded, killing Ruhl instantly, but Hank was saved.

The Japanese were still throwing grenades, so Lieutenant Wells ordered Sergeant Snyder forward to hurl grenades into the fleeing soldiers while Robeson and Adrian opened fire with their rifles. Snyder quickly ran out of grenades, so Wells threw his own to the sergeant.

There were so many enemies to fight that the Marines were quickly running out of ammunition, so Wells sent Corporal Wayne Hathaway and Edward Krisik back to headquarters to bring up more ammunition, charges, and grenades. The men dashed back toward headquarters, but they never made it back. Both were mortally wounded on the way by Japanese fire.

Meanwhile mortars continued to explode among the men of Boots' platoon and the chatter of machine gun fire filled the air. The men fired as best as they could, but without the help of tanks they couldn't silence the enemy positions. Soon Louie Adrian, another member of the platoon, fell dead, shot through the heart.

The small platoon was battling Japanese in front of them as well as to their left and right where the enemy was protected in their large blockhouse and other defensive positions. Marines from Company I were supposed to be helping the men of Lieutenant Wells' platoon, but somehow Company I hadn't reached the mountain yet. Lieutenant Wells knew that his men would all be killed if the other Marines didn't arrive, so he sent Sergeant Boots back to find them and to lead them forward.

The Japanese fire around the mountain was intense and deadly. Boots could see that his men wouldn't live much longer without help. He later wrote: "we lost 17 men out of 46" on that morning.[37]

Soon after Boots left, Lieutenant Wells dove into a bomb crater to protect himself from the Japanese gunners while he made a phone call back to headquarters to let Captain Severance know what was happening. Four other men from the platoon were in the crater with him.

Just as Lieutenant Wells finished the call a mortar landed behind him and exploded. All five men were wounded. Lieutenant Wells received deep leg injuries and wasn't sure that he could continue in the battle, but he knew that he had to keep leading his men.

Just then Chuck Lindberg and Robert Goode, the platoon's flamethrowers, arrived. Lieutenant Wells sent them forward to attack the pillbox to their left, where the Japanese were firing at them with machine guns. Chuck quickly killed the enemies inside the pillbox and moved on to the next target. With his large flamethrower tank on his back he knew that he was an easy target for the Japanese gunners, but he didn't seem to care. He knew that he had a job to do, and he intended to see it done.

Even though Chuck had silenced the pillbox, the Japanese in the large concrete blockhouse to their right were hurling a steady stream of grenades into the midst of the platoon. The Marines weren't able to defend themselves against the Japanese inside the blockhouse because of the thick concrete walls protecting the defenders. On the opposite side of the blockhouse was a large machine gun which was spouting out a deadly stream of bullets, killing many Marines who were rushing forward to attack it. It seemed impossible to stop the Japanese inside the blockhouse.

While Lieutenant Wells watched the fire from the blockhouse and wondered what to do, he heard a shout behind him and turned to see what it meant. Looking around, he saw in amazement and joy that two tanks were drawing near! At last help had arrived! As he watched one of the tanks turned toward him, and Lieutenant Wells saw that it was being led by Sergeant Boots Thomas.

Boots led the tank to the platoon's side and quickly pointed out the enemy blockhouse that was killing so many men. Aiming at point-blank range, the tank fired nineteen shells into the concrete walls before it was able to break through them so that the Marines could kill the enemy defenders.

After silencing the blockhouse, Boots and Hank Hansen led the tanks forward to other Japanese strongholds and began clearing the area of the enemy. With the tanks' fire support, Boots and his Marines soon captured the ground in front of them and were able to advance toward the mountain.

While Boots worked with the tanks, Lieutenant Wells realized that his wounds were so severe that he couldn't

USMC

continue leading his platoon any longer. He called Boots and gave him complete charge of the men, and then turned back and headed for the rear. His legs were so badly wounded that he couldn't walk far, so he crawled to an aid station. From there he was carried on a stretcher to the beach and evacuated to a hospital ship. He had bravely led his platoon against Mount Suribachi that morning, but for the moment his fighting was over.

Now in charge of the platoon, Boots continued to lead his men forward against the defense positions surrounding the base of Suribachi. The Japanese positions were so well built that the men of the platoon weren't able to beat them. Boots quickly realized that he would need more tank support before his men could move forward. He therefore left his men

USMC
204535-5

in a protected position and ran back to the nearest tank.

The tanks were a wonderful help in battle, but the men inside the tanks weren't able to see where the Japanese defense positions were located. They needed a Marine to stand outside the tank and point out where they should fire. Boots knew this, so he stood in front of the tank and pointed out the enemy positions that were attacking his men.

Boots' position in front of the tank was immediately noticed by the enemy, who instantly aimed their fire at him. The Japanese knew that the tanks would be useless if someone didn't show them where to shoot, so they worked furiously to kill any soldier who tried to show the tank crew where to direct their fire.

Boots knew he was in a dangerous position, but he didn't care. He had to protect his men, and to do that he needed the tank's help. Fearlessly he stood and pointed out the Japanese pillboxes and blockhouses. Then, after the tanks had successfully destroyed the positions, Boots ran back to his platoon and led his men forward in an assault against the new ground.

After they had moved forward, Boots and his platoon again found themselves stuck while new Japanese positions opened up in front of them. Boots left his men in their craters and shell holes and again dashed back across the open ground raked by machine guns and mortars. He found another tank and led it forward to attack the Japanese who were blocking his men's advance. Boots stood in front of the tank's turret and pointed out the location of the Japanese positions with his rifle, and again the defenses were soon demolished by the tank's fire.

Again and again throughout the battle Boots repeated these moves, directing the tanks and then racing back to his men to lead them forward against each new position. The Japanese snipers tried again and again to kill him. At last they succeeded in shooting the rifle he carried in his hand. The rifle was destroyed, and Boots realized that he had almost been killed. But he didn't care; he knew he had to protect his men, so he threw his rifle away and pulled out his knife. With the knife Boots continued to point out the Japanese positions to the tanks.

The men of Boots' platoon watched their leader's bravery and were inspired to work even harder to win against the Japanese. With Boots' leadership they were finally able to break through the Japanese defenses and make their way up to the base of Mount Suribachi. Richard Wheeler, one of the men of the platoon, wrote about Boots: "It was he who discovered the soft spot in the belt of defenses . . . He himself led the breakthrough."[38]

Captain Severance watched Boots as he led his men forward and was thankful to have such a man leading the men. He wrote about Boots: "He was one of the few born leaders of men I have met."[39]

Finally, after hours of desperate fighting around the base of the mountain, the Marines surrounding Suribachi were finally stopped by the setting of the sun.

With the coming of darkness Boots gathered his men in preparation for whatever the night might hold. The day's fighting had been costly. Almost half the members of his platoon were dead or wounded. Boots organized the remaining men on their newly-won ground and prepared for the night. He and his Marines were now so close to the mountain that they could hear the Japanese talking in their tunnels and caves deep inside Suribachi.

As they settled in for the night, the men thought over what had happened during the day and how many men they had lost. Many of their comrades (and their lieutenant) were on hospital ships or were lying dead waiting to be buried. As the darkness descended Hank Hansen thought again about how Donald Ruhl had saved his life. Truly Ruhl had displayed the "greater love" the Bible talks about that shows itself in deeds and actions rather than only in words (John 15:13; I John 3:18).

CHAPTER TWENTY

Raising Old Glory

February 22 dawned drearily. A cold, driving rain greeted the weary Marines as they prepared for another day of grappling with the mountain. Sergeant Boots and his men were now located at the very base of Suribachi, and throughout the day Boots led his men in an attack against the remaining enemy positions surrounding them. They hoped to destroy as many pillboxes and blockhouses as possible because tomorrow they were scheduled to begin their attack on the mountain itself.

With the arrival of dawn on February 23 Boots and his men prepared to attack Mount Suribachi. Before the Marines moved forward Navy planes swooped low overhead to drop their bombs on the mountain. The planes hoped to destroy some of the Japanese defense positions before the Marines began their assault.

The hum of the approaching plane engines was a welcome sound to the waiting Marines, but soon the noise drew too near for comfort. Confused, the planes mistook their target and began dropping their bombs on the American lines of Marines. Boots and his men ran for cover while Captain Severance radioed the fleet in a frantic effort to end the bombing and save his men.

The men on the other end of the radio wouldn't listen to Captain Severance. But, providentially, the battalion commander heard Captain Severance's call for help and stopped the bombing.

USMC

After the planes departed, a four-man patrol was sent up the mountain on reconnaissance. It didn't encounter any resistance from the Japanese and was able to climb to the summit and back without injury. The Marines assumed that the Japanese were hiding until the main force of the Americans began ascending the mountain, so Captain Severance called Boots' platoon over and told them to climb to the top of Suribachi.

Boots only had twenty-five men left in his platoon, so Captain Severance added fifteen more men from other platoons and assigned Lieutenant Harold Shrier to command the men. Each of the Marines were given extra grenades and ammunition, and two teams of stretcher bearers were added to carry down the wounded. The platoon was also accompanied by Sergeant Louis Lowery, a photographer.

Before the platoon began its ascent Colonel Johnson

**Colonel Johnson talking on the phone with
Suribachi in the background**

handed Lieutenant Schrier a small American flag and told him: "If you get to the top, put this up."

Captain Severance silently watched the men leave and wondered if any of them would come back alive. He wrote: "I thought I was sending those men to their deaths."[40]

Silently Lieutenant Schrier, Sergeant Boots, and their men approached the mountain. Its steep volcanic sides were difficult to climb, but the men carefully picked their way along and slowly ascended its rocky slopes. Sometimes the way was so steep that the men climbed on hands and knees to reach the top.

To the platoon's astonishment, no enemy appeared as they climbed the mountain. Sergeant Boots was surprised at this. He explained:

In fact, not a single shot was fired at us all the way up

the side of the mountain, and we didn't lose a man—
although we passed a lot of pillboxes on the way, and
Japs were found in them later. I think the naval gunfire
and the blasting from artillery and bombs must have
buried a lot of them and pinned the others down.[41]

After a difficult half-hour climb the platoon reached
the rim of the crater at the top of the volcano. Schrier called
a halt as he and Boots examined the situation. Boots looked
around and saw that the Japanese had carefully prepared their
defenses on the top of the mountain. He noted: "There was
a whole battery of heavy Japanese machine guns around the
rim of the volcano. They seemed to be all ready for use, with
ammunition stacked around them and magazines alongside."[42]
But, even though the defense positions were built and ready to
use, there were no Japanese to be seen anywhere.

USMC

Schrier and Boots led their men around the rim of the crater to the summit of the volcano. From there they fanned out into the crater and began looking for the enemy. Boots noted the first person to find them:

> Clarence Garrett sighted a Jap in a kind of combination cave and observation post off to the left. So while Lt. Schrier got the flag ready and one squad stood guard, the other two moved over there. We got three of them in that cave.[43]

The Marines quickly fought off the few Japanese who appeared on top of the mountain. Then they began putting up the flag that the colonel had sent with them. Someone found a piece of Japanese pipe to use as a flagpole. Then Schrier and Boots, accompanied by Hansen and Lindberg, tied the flag to

Left to right:
**Schrier, Boots, Hansen, and Lindberg
attach flag to Japanese pipe**

Sergeant Boots Thomas stands in front of flag

the pipe and, raising it carefully in the strong wind, secured it in the volcano's rugged ground by piling rocks around its base. The photographer Lowery pulled out his camera and quickly snapped a few pictures while the flag was being raised.

As soon as the flag was up, more Japanese crept out of their caves and tunnels to attack the Marines and try to pull down the flag. One of the Japanese riflemen shot at Chick Robeson and Lowery, but Robeson quickly killed him. Another Japanese rushed out with a raised saber, but was also killed by the platoon's riflemen.

Soon shots and grenades were coming from several different directions. Dashing for cover, the Marines returned the Japanese fire and a fight ensued. Lou Lowery, the photographer, had climbed the mountain without a weapon. Now he found himself in a firefight unable to defend himself. One of the Japanese saw him and threw a grenade in his direction. Lowery jumped out of the way of the grenade—and fell right off the top of the mountain.

Lowry rolled thirty or forty feet down the steep slope before he could catch himself. When he finally stopped and caught his breath he realized that he wasn't hurt, but his camera had been crushed by the fall. Lowery was glad that the film was still safe, but he decided that it was time for him to head back to safety, so he started down the mountain to find a new camera.

While Lieutenant Schrier and Sergeant Boots were leading their platoon up the rugged sides of the volcano, they didn't realize that they were being watched by countless eyes. From the Marines on the beaches to the sailors gathered on the ships in the fleet, hundreds of men had caught the movement of the small patrol as it began its ascent up the mountain, and they watched breathlessly to see what would happen to them. Marines on shore strained to see while ships' crews peered through binoculars as Boots' men climbed higher and higher up the steep slopes.

When at last the platoon had reached the top of the

mountain, they disappeared from view as they passed over the summit into the crater below. The men below watched and waited in suspense while they wondered if any of the Marines would live to reappear on the crater's edge.

Then, suddenly, a distant speck of red, white, and blue appeared on top of the mountain and a cry went up across the island: "There goes the flag!" In an instant the ground at the base of Suribachi erupted in shouts of joy as Marines waved their hats and rifles and yelled, while others stood silently as tears of joy slipped down their faces.

The men on the landing beaches saw the flag as well. Corporal Hershel Williams was standing on the beaches and remembered:

> People around me started yelling and screaming and jumping up and down and firing their weapons, and for a few seconds I couldn't tell what in the world was going on. And then I looked up and saw Old Glory flying above Mount Suribachi, so I just joined and fired mine too. I jumped up and down and screamed.[44]

The fight for Iwo Jima wasn't over yet, but the view of Old Glory waving proudly from Suribachi inspired the hearts of all who saw it, and the cry which had risen on the island soon echoed beyond its beaches. Across the water the rejoicing continued, where men with binoculars had breathlessly watched the platoon's tense climb up the volcano. Bells, whistles, and horns sounded on the ships when the tiny Stars and Stripes were raised on top of the mountain. Sailors at the rails jumped up and down and cheered while the ships' loudspeakers announced the joyful news to the wounded Marines lying in their hospital cots.

General Holland Smith had just landed on the beach when the flag was raised. James Forrestal, the secretary of the navy, was also with him, and was excited to see the flag flying so high above them. He was so happy about the flag-raising that he decided he would like to take the flag home as a souvenir.

When Colonel Johnson, Boots' colonel, heard that Mr. Forrestal wanted the flag, he wasn't happy. He wanted the Marines to keep the flag, so he sent a new flag up the mountain and told the men to raise it instead so that they could give it to Mr. Forrestal.

Meanwhile Boots and his platoon were still at work on top of the mountain fighting the Japanese. Boots was standing on the summit with some of his men when a Japanese machine gun appeared and began firing at them. The Marines dashed for cover and began firing back when they suddenly heard more firing. To their surprise they saw another company of Marines on their way up the mountain. The extra men had been sent up to help Boots and his platoon, and they were able to stop the machine gunner as they reached the top of the

USMC

First flag is lowered as second flag is raised

USMC

Schrier and Boots salute the flag

mountain. Soon things began to quiet down as the Marines fought off the last of the Japanese defenders.

Before long another group of Marines reached the top of Suribachi. They had been sent by Colonel Johnson to raise the second flag. The pole the men found for the second flag was so heavy that it took six men to raise it. Schrier, Boots, and a few of their men lowered the first flag while Michael Strank, Franklin Sousley, Ira Hayes, Harold Schultz, Rene

Gagnon, and Corporal Harlon Block raised the second flag. Joe Rosenthal and Robert Campbell, two photographers, and Sergeant William Genaust (who had brought a video camera) all took pictures as the flag went up.

After the second flag was raised the photographers took more pictures and then headed back down the mountain. The afternoon was beginning to wear away, so Schrier and Boots established their men in a defensive position in preparation for the coming night. Now that they had captured the top of the mountain, they had to defend it from all the Japanese soldiers still living in caves and tunnels inside the mountain. Boots wondered whether the Japanese would attack them during the night. He later remembered: "We stayed there all night, but nobody slept very much."[45]

CHAPTER TWENTY-ONE

Meeting a Reporter

Finally the tense night passed away, and again the dawn welcomed the weary Marines to another day on the island. Now that they had captured the mountain, Boots' platoon and the other Marines of the 28th Regiment spent the morning clearing the caves along the rim and sides of the mountain. To their surprise it turned out to be an easier job than they had thought it would be, and the men enjoyed a relatively quiet day on the volcano.

While the Marines had been fighting on Iwo Jima, news of their battle on the little island had been radioed back to the United States. People there were listening eagerly for news to hear how the battle was progressing. When news arrived that Suribachi had been taken, everyone wanted to hear more about it. Therefore an order from the fleet was sent to Boots and his platoon on the mountain. A radioman on Admiral Kelly Turner's flagship wanted to interview one of the Marines about the volcano and the flag-raising.

Lieutenant Schrier received the request and decided to send Boots to the ship since he had led the platoon in their attack against the mountain. Boots therefore scrambled back down Suribachi and made his way to the beach to be transported to the fleet's flagship for an interview.

Arriving at the ship, Sergeant Boots was greeted by Don Pryor, a CBS news correspondent. Boots was exhausted after ten days of non-stop fighting. He had barely slept at all since he'd landed on Iwo Jima and he was still covered with dust and dirt from the battle, but Mr. Pryor didn't mind. He sat down with the young Marine and began interviewing him over the radio. He began by saying:

> This is Don Pryor on the flying bridge of Admiral Turner's flagship off the coast of Iwo Jima. And here beside me is the leader of the Marine platoon from the Fifth Division which raised the American flag high on the top of Suribachi Volcano at the southern tip of Iwo Jima. He is Platoon Sergeant Ernest I. Thomas, a modest but tough 20-year-old fighting man from Tallahassee, Florida. Sergeant, you are the first American in history who has ever raised Old Glory over a part of the Japanese home empire.[46]

Mr. Pryor turned to Boots and was surprised when Boots shook his head in disagreement. Stunned, Sergeant Boots realized that Mr. Pryor's opening statement had said that he was the man responsible for raising the flag. Yet Boots wasn't the only person responsible for capturing the mountain and raising the flag. He knew that all his men had as big a part in it as he did.

Boots didn't want to be rude to the reporter, but he knew he had to correct him, so he leaned forward and said: "No, Mr. Pryor—I don't want to give that impression. The honor belongs to every man in my platoon."

Boots quickly set the record straight by listing the names of the men of his platoon who had physically raised the flag. "But," he added, "the rest of the men had just as big a part in it as we did."

"How did you feel about it?" Mr. Pryor asked.

"Well," Boots replied, "to tell the truth, we didn't have time to think about it. Later, of course, when we had everything more or less secure and we watched it whipping up there in the wind, we felt mighty proud. But our chief worry right then was how to defend it."

USMC

Carrying the flag up Suribachi

Mr. Pryor next asked about the Japanese resistance which met the platoon. Boots answered that the number of the enemy they found wasn't as many as they had expected. He explained that reaching the top of Suribachi had been much easier than they thought it would be, though once they got to the top the platoon had quickly run into the enemy waiting for them.

Sgt. Boots Thomas shakes hands with General Smith

"Was there any ceremony when you raised the flag?" asked Mr. Pryor.

"No," Boots replied. "We were in too much of a hurry. Before we started up the mountain, Lt.-Col. Chandler W. Johnson, our battalion commander, handed the flag to Lt. Schrier—all rolled up, and said, 'Put that on top of the hill.' And the lieutenant said, 'Okay.' When we got there we put it up, on a flag pole made out of a piece of Japanese pipe. And then we got busy, mopping up our side of the mountain and sending out patrols."

Pryor ended the interview by asking the weary Marine, "How long has it been since you've had a night's sleep?"

"A real night's sleep, you mean?" Boots asked. "I can't remember."

"Well, I think you've done your share for a few hours," Mr. Pryor replied. "And since you'll be going back again before long, why don't you go to bed?"

Turning back to his radio audience, the newsman continued: "You have just heard an interview with Sergeant Ernest I. "Tommy" Thomas of Tallahassee, Florida, who led a Marine platoon to the top of Suribachi Volcano and helped raise the first American flag ever to fly above any part of the Japanese home empire. This is Don Pryor, representing the combined American radio networks. I return you to the United States."

Mr. Pryor was surprised at how mature Boots was for being only twenty years old. It also surprised him that Boots had been so careful to be sure that all his men received credit for raising the flag. He wrote about Boots: "My interest in him swiftly became much more than impersonal, and my respect and admiration for him were very great."[47]

When all the interviews were finished General Holland Smith had his picture taken with Sergeant Boots. Then Boots headed back to Iwo Jima to rejoin his men and continue the battle against the Japanese.

CHAPTER TWENTY-TWO

Excitement at Home

On February 20th, just twenty-four hours after the Marines first set foot on the beaches of Iwo Jima, Mrs. Thomas sat down to write her son. "I wish you could have been home this week-end," she began, but then wrote:

> I'm glad now that I don't know where you are. I think I would go crazy if I knew.
>
> I had a letter from Jim the other day—he said he would be home in three weeks, and that he would certainly be right over to see me just as soon as he got home.
>
> Darling, remember I love you and miss you more every day. And do write if it's possible.
>
> All my love,
> Mother[48]

Before long Mrs. Thomas would learn that her son was one of the thousands of Marines fighting on Iwo Jima. The Tallahassee paper that morning had recorded the start of the battle for that island. Then, five days later, newspapers across the country printed a picture of Marines raising a flag on top of Mount Suribachi. Beneath the picture they printed the exciting story:

> Five days, one hour and 30 minutes after American Marines of the Fifth division waded across the black

beaches of the southern end of this island, the American flag flew for the first time from the summit of the 556-foot crater Suribachi Yama.

This bloody battle for Iwo Jima is far from over, but the weary Marines with the biggest part of the job still ahead of them took heart at the sight of their flag flying above them.

They had the added knowledge it was flying for the first time only 660 air miles from the Japanese mainland.

. . . the flag was planted atop Suribachi by Platoon Sergeant Ernest Ivy Thomas, Jr., of Tallahassee, Fla.[49]

General Smith and Sgt. Boots Thomas

In surprise and excitement Mrs. Thomas read the newspaper and rejoiced to finally hear news of her son. "Just to know that he is still alive is all I can think of!" she exclaimed.[50] That evening she sat down to write Boots:

Sunday night
February 25, 1945
Darling, Darling,

What am I ever going to do with you? I knew darling that you would do something wonderful. And I'm so proud of you. You know that, though—you have never had to climb volcanoes for me to know just how wonderful you are.

Tallahassee is just wild over the news—"Our own Ernest I. Thomas, Jr."—Tampa with a perfect right is claiming you, too—the whole of Monticello was waiting to hear your broadcast this afternoon—also Tampa— and Jim Lawrence at Gainesville. Mother Thomas just wept when I called her. The phone has been ringing all day and last night. We got the first word last night over the radio. They wanted me to speak over the radio this afternoon on a Red Cross programme, but I just couldn't today. But I am Wednesday.

Calls have been coming in from everywhere. Washington, Jacksonville, Tampa, Gainesville. Your picture with the flag was in the Tampa Tribune this morning. The original is going to be sent me from Washington. I'm saving all the clippings—wires and everything for you.[51]

In closing Mrs. Thomas voiced her greatest desire for young Boots: "If I could only see you and tell you to be more careful. It isn't the glory I want. I want you to come back."

"My prayers are with you, darling," she concluded, "and I feel so sure that you will come out all right. Jack and Jean are simply thrilled—and I love you, darling. Will write again tomorrow. All my love, Mother."

Newspapers across the country honor Boots

CHAPTER TWENTY-THREE

Leading His Men

While Boots made his way back across the island of Iwo Jima to join his men, he had no idea that he was being thought of by so many people across the nation back home. In Texas Jim Sledge was just finishing up his training with the Air Corps and sat down to write a quick note to Boots on the 28th of February:

Dear Boots,

Just got a letter from home and they told me about you. [They sent] a clipping about you sending the flag up at Iwo. Sure was good to find out where you are, and that you were OK.

Say, boy, haven't you gotten any of my letters? I've written several times, but not a word from you. Guess you're pretty busy, but how about a line?

Just one more week here before we graduate. Guess I'll be by to see your mother then. I'm not sure how long it will be 'fore we have a chance to leave, but I'm pretty anxious.

There's not much news here, but thought I'd write. Drop a line when you can.

Tú amigo,
Jim[52]

Meanwhile Boots and his platoon had been reassigned. Leaving Mount Suribachi, they moved north across the island

THE MUSCATINE JOURNAL

MUSCATINE—LOG FORT CITY OF THE CORN BELT

MUSCATINE, IOWA, WEDNESDAY, MARCH 7, 1945 — TWELVE PAGES — ESTABLISHED 1840

ASSOCIATED PRESS and NEA SERVICE

FIVE CENTS A COPY

Red Forces Assault Kuestrin

Yanks 15 Miles South Of Fallen Cologne

Routed Nazis Flee Toward Middle Rhine

Internal Uprisings In Italy, Romania Worry To Diplomats

Allies In Italy Gain Five Miles

Russians Attack On Both Sides Of Town After 24 Hour Barrage, Nazis Say

Ohio River In Slow But Steady Rise

Widespread Air Attacks Pound Reich

Launch Offensive To Push Japs From Iwo

Weather Delays Canvassing For Red Cross Drive

Conferees Group Eyes Workmen's Compensation Act

THE MONTICELLO NEWS

THE RED CLAY HILL SECTION OF FLORIDA

JEFFERSON COUNTY

MONTICELLO, FLORIDA, FRIDAY, MARCH 9, 1945

FLORIDA'S IDEAL FARMING AND DAIRYING SECTION

FIVE CENTS A COPY

mbley Plead rged In Shooting elts Was Fired Upon

Red Cross War Fund eeds Your Help In Raising $4,000 Goal

Womans Club Meeting

Director Kennedy Tells Of Operation Of Game Department

Property Transfers In County In 1944 Show Big Increase

Marine Hero Who Raised Old Glory On Crater Top of Iwo Jima Is Our Own Boots Thomas—M.H.S. Graduate

Post-Auxiliary Meeting

27 Years Ago

ITEMS FORM THE MONTICELLO NEWS MARCH 1, 1918

Thomasville Times-Enterprise

THOMASVILLE, MONDAY, FEBRUARY 19, 1945

U.S. 9TH BREAKS THRU GERMAN DEFENSES
RUSSIANS GAIN IN BALTIC AND ON NIESSE

AMERICANS AT ERFT RIVER IN TEN-MILE ADVANCE WEST OF URDB, ENTER KONIGSHOVEN

BRITSH ACCEPTS SENATE VERSION OF CONSTITUTION

U.S. SUBS TURNED DOWN 12 DISTINCT JAP PEACE BIDS

BREAK THROUGH FOR 30 MILES IN POMERANIA IN EFFORT TO ISOLATE BIG AREA FROM REICH

TWO JAP AIRCRAFT FACTORIES DAMAGED, 223 PLANES BLASTED

VESSELS HIT BY AMERICANS

Churchill Declares Big Three Prepared For German Collapse

MANILA GIVEN CIVIL STATUS BY MACARTHUR

BRITISH LEADER HAS FAITH IN RUSSIA'S WILLINGNESS TO AID IN PLANS FOR PEACE

NEW CONSTRUCTION WILL ADD 550 BEDS TO FINNEY HOSPITAL

COL. S. M. BROWNE ANNOUNCES CONSTRUCTION OF BARRACKS GETS UNDERWAY AT ONCE

and joined the Marines fighting the Japanese in the northern heights of Iwo Jima. Because Lieutenant Wells' wounds were so serious he still wasn't able to lead his men, so command of the platoon was again given to Boots.

The Marines under Boots Thomas hardly resembled the group of forty-six hearty men that had landed on the beaches of Iwo Jima only eleven days previously. They were now wearied and bloodied, battle-worn and exhausted. As Boots looked them over he was saddened to think of how many men were missing. Ruhl was dead. Romero was dead. Lieutenant Wells, Corporal Wheeler, Ed Kurelik, and others had been evacuated due to their wounds—and the battle for Iwo Jima had only begun.

The new ground in the north that the Marines needed to capture from the Japanese was every bit as deadly as the ground they had taken at the base of Suribachi. Jagged hills and rocky ravines met the Marines' eyes. More bunkers, pillboxes, blockhouses, and machine gun nests were hiding along the ridges and elevated heights of the northern hills. Hundreds of Marines had already died while fighting for this ground, and many, many more would fall before the men won the day.

Boots and his platoon joined the Marines in the north just as they were moving against a large rocky mass called Hill 362A. It was one of the highest elevations on that end of the island and was one of the main strong points of the Japanese northern defenses. Its sides were covered with caves and defensive positions. Tunnels cut through its interior, allowing the Japanese to easily and safely move back and forth between their positions.

After examining Hill 362A, Boots knew he would probably be leading his men to their deaths.

"My twenty-first birthday is coming up March 10," he muttered, "but I'll never see it."[53]

Before dawn the Marines moved into place in preparation for the attack. At 6:30 A.M. the 5th Division's

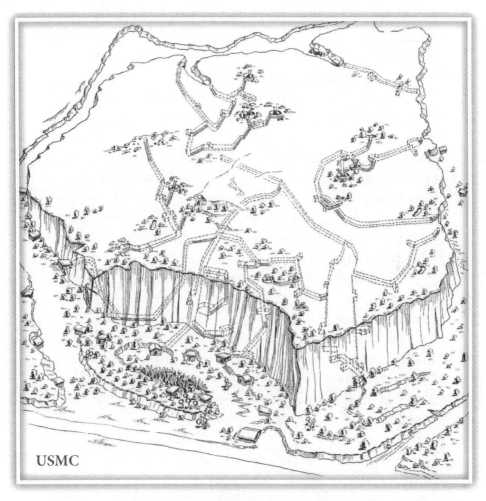

USMC

Hill 362A
(dotted lines indicate Japanese tunnels)

artillery opened fire on the hill. A battleship and two cruisers from the fleet added their guns to the bombardment. Then, as soon as the guns fell silent, the Marines of the 28th began the attack. Leading his platoon, Boots pressed forward with the rest of his regiment toward the rocky hill.

Japanese mortar and small-arms fire prevented the Marines from getting very far, and casualties in Boots' platoon began immediately. Robert Leader, one of the men who had helped find the flagpole on top of Suribachi, was shot and evacuated. Shortly afterward Sergeant Hank Hansen, whose life had been saved several days earlier by Donald Ruhl, was also shot and killed.

For over an hour the Marines battled their way up the bloody sides of Hill 362A. Finally they reached the summit. But, to their dismay, this didn't bring them much help. The other side of Hill 362A was a sheer cliff, and the Marines had no way of getting down to the ravine below. They also found themselves under fire from another ridge a few hundred yards to the north. From this position (known as Nishi Ridge), the Japanese had a clear view of the Marines on top of Hill 362A and easily mowed them down with their rifle fire and mortars.

Sergeant Boots continued to lead his Marines against the bloody hill, but the men were dropping quickly. The next man to fall was Chuck Lindberg, the flamethrower. Lindberg recalls the afternoon's fighting:

> I was trying to get to a mortar position, kind of running across the side of a ridge there, and all of a sudden—*boom!*—a bullet went right straight through my right forearm and on through my jacket. I was bent over like this, and if I'd been standing straight, another inch or two, it would have got me. . . . It shattered my forearm bone.[54]

Lindberg's wound was treated by Bradley, the platoon's corpsman, and the wounded flamethrower was ordered to the rear. He hated to leave the other Marines, but knew that he wouldn't be any good in the fight with only one arm.

At last the setting sun put an end to the day's fighting and men dug in for the night wherever they could find any type of shelter. They had managed to capture the Hill, but Nishi Ridge and the ravine in between were still in enemy hands.

With night approaching Boots quietly looked over the tattered remnants of his platoon. Easy Company had suffered

USMC

38 casualties in the day's battle. Many more faces were missing and many new graves were being dug in the Marine cemetery behind the lines.

When the dawn of March 2 arrived the Marines again readied themselves for a forward advance. They spent the day battling for the ravine behind Hill 362A and destroying the numerous defenses along the cliff face.

Enemy fire roared from every direction as Boots led his men into the ravine. Heavy artillery from the distant Nishi Ridge crashed among them and small-arms and mortar fire poured in from the open ground ahead of them. Behind them a hail of bullets and grenades issued from the openings in the cliff face at the back of Hill 362A. Undaunted, Sergeant Boots brought his men into position and, with the other Marines

USMC

USMC

Colonel Chandler Johnson

of Easy Company, systematically began destroying the enemy positions blocking their advance.   Armored tanks, with assistance from the Marines on the ground, also directed their fire against the Japanese positions built into the cliff face.

It was a bloody fight for the ravine, but by afternoon the Marines had broken through and were pushing ahead across the open ground toward Nishi Ridge. They hoped to attack Nishi Ridge the next morning.

During a lull in the afternoon fighting Colonel Chandler Johnson, Boots' battalion commander, advanced toward Easy Company's new command post. The colonel was very proud when he heard that his Marines were the first to touch Nishi Ridge, and he decided to visit them to congratulate them in person. As he stepped out of his jeep to talk to his men, however, an artillery shell struck him, killing him instantly.

Shocked and saddened, with heavy hearts the men of Easy Company dug in for the night at the base of Nishi Ridge. They hoped to take the ridge in the morning, but how many more of them would die fighting before it was all over?

Boots and the few men of his platoon still left alive burrowed into their foxholes as darkness settled in that evening. In the quiet stillness that came with the setting sun Boots pictured the ridge in his mind and thought about how he would attack it in the morning. He knew that the lives of the men lying beside him were in his hands, and the weight of those lives rested heavily on his young shoulders. His Marines had complete confidence in their leader, and they were counting on Boots to lead them through the next day's fighting. They didn't know how they would take the ridge, but they trusted Boots and knew that their fearless sergeant would find a way through the coming battle. The knowledge that his men were relying on him to find the best way to win the battle and keep them alive kept twenty-year-old Boots awake as darkness fell.

Darkness settled over the island and the Marines hoped to catch a little sleep before the next day arrived. Then, suddenly, a cry went up. The Japanese were attacking! From Hill 362A fifty Japanese soldiers crept out of their caves and raced to the Marines lying on the ground in front of Nishi Ridge. Concealed by the darkness, the Japanese attacked the startled Marines and a hand-to-hand battle began. The Marines fought desperately and finally overcame the Japanese attack, but after the fighting ended nobody thought about going to sleep anymore.

At last the morning arrived and the Marines prepared for their next attack. Boots, after studying the ground they'd be taking, turned to his men.

USMC

"It's going to be rough going over there," he admitted.[55]

But, no matter how difficult it was, Boots knew his men would give all they had, and at 7:45 A.M. Sergeant Boots left his foxhole and darted forward, leading his men in the attack on Nishi Ridge.

Heavy mortar fire met the Marines of the 28th Regiment, but the men pressed onward, painfully and slowly, as they led the attack on the ridge.

Boots' men hadn't gone far before they found themselves surrounded by rifle fire from several hidden Japanese positions. As his men ducked for cover, Sergeant Boots saw that their right flank was exposed to enemy fire because the Marines of Company D, who had been advancing to their right, had been delayed by heavy mortar fire.

Boots knew that his platoon would be immediately killed if they moved forward without assistance on their right, so he stopped beside a rock and picked up the field telephone. Contacting the command post, he asked them to send support for his men so that they could continue the advance.

While Boots talked on the phone, the Japanese around him were watching. Talking on the telephone marked Boots as a leader, and the Japanese aimed their fire at him in an attempt to kill him. Boots immediately found bullets whistling past his ears as he made his call. His rifle was quickly knocked out of his hand by the enemy's fire, but Boots paid no attention to it and continued to request support for his men. It was only a moment, however, before the Japanese aim proved true. A few seconds after his rifle was shot from his hand, a second bullet found its mark and killed Boots instantly.

USMC

In shock Boots' men watched their leader fall. For almost two weeks he had fearlessly led them through countless dangers and difficulties, and now—in a split second—he was gone.

The reality of Boots' death was hard for his men to grasp, but there wasn't time to mourn for him. The attack had to move on, so Boots' men mixed themselves with the other Marines of Easy Company and continued the advance against Nishi Ridge. They would capture the ridge before long, but many more Marines would be lying cold beside Boots before the battle had been won.

The date was March the 3rd. More than three weeks of intense fighting remained before the Americans won the fight for little Iwo Jima. By the end of the battle for the volcanic island Boots' platoon would almost cease to exist. Of its original 46 men, only four would leave the island unharmed.

Even as the Marines continued their attack in the north, other Marines were busy in the south creating cemeteries to begin burying their comrades who had fallen in the fight. The cemeteries would contain over six thousand bodies before the battle was won.

The body of Platoon Sergeant Ernest Boots Thomas, Jr. was carried behind the lines and buried in the Division cemetery in Plot 5, Row 19, Grave 1376, and a telegram was sent to his mother in Florida:

DEEPLY REGRET TO INFORM YOU THAT YOUR SON SERGEANT ERNEST I THOMAS JR USMCR WAS KILLED IN ACTION ON 3 MARCH 1945 AT IWO JIMA VOLCANO ISLANDS IN THE PERFORMANCE OF HIS DUTY AND SERVICE OF HIS COUNTRY.[56]

In shock and disbelief Mrs. Thomas read the telegram, and wept. Could it be true? After all that had happened, could Boots really be gone?

With a broken heart Mrs. Thomas dropped the telegram and turned away. It was true. Her dearest son wasn't coming home.

Jim Sledge had just graduated from his Army Air Corps training in Texas when he also heard the dreadful news. On that faraway island in the Pacific his best friend had just been killed. It was hard to believe that Boots was dead, but sadly Jim realized that he would never see his friend again.

Fifth Marine Division Cemetery on Iwo Jima

CHAPTER TWENTY-FOUR

An Invisible Hero

Now that his training was finished, Jim was scheduled to ship out in the beginning of August to join in the war against the Japanese. But, just before he left the States, he received news that Japan was ready to surrender. After four years of fighting, America's war with Japan was finally over.

When the Japanese surrendered Jim's Uncle Teddy was released from prison camp and was flown home to be with his family. He had suffered much during his long years as a prisoner of war and was in bad shape when he reached America, but he was alive and thankful to be on his way home once again. Jim and his family were overjoyed to have him back safely, and Jim flew out to San Francisco to welcome him back to the States.

After the war Jim Sledge returned to Monticello. In 1947 the Marine Corps flew Boots' body home to Monticello as well and it was buried in the Monticello cemetery alongside his father.

With Boots dead, the boys' childhood dream of earning a fortune in South America no longer sounded exciting, so Jim instead settled on a profession in

Uncle Teddy after the war

dentistry, and in 1952 he opened a dental practice in town.

Little had changed in Monticello when Jim reentered the town after the war. The old streets were still the same, the local businesses had scarcely changed, and the majestic courthouse still rose silently to crown the rural country landscape.

All outwardly appeared unchanged in quiet Monticello, but to Jim a sad emptiness filled the pleasant scene. The fresh grave in the local cemetery now cast a solemn gloom over his boyhood home. As he walked Monticello's streets tears slipped silently down his cheeks as his ears unconsciously strained to hear the well-known sounds of Boots' familiar voice.

Meeting schoolmates and old friends again was a pleasure for Jim, but Boots' absence from the old familiar places was difficult for him to bear. "I couldn't even say the name Boots Thomas without breaking down," he recalled. "I just couldn't talk about it."[57]   For him the grief was still too fresh.

Many within the little town shared Jim's sorrow. Over a dozen local boys had not returned from the war, and over a dozen graves remained the only markers of youthful lives lost.

Now that the war was over, however, the town began to return to life as usual. Jim settled into his dental practice and started a family. Boots' siblings Jack and Jean Thomas both married and began families as well, and the world moved on.

Though at first unable to speak about Boots, Jim's love for his friend never faded, and as the years went by he realized that he couldn't remain silent about Boots' life and death. A new generation of young people was rising up, and that generation didn't know who Boots was and would never hear his story unless someone told them.

When the war began on December 7, 1941, Boots recognized that he had a role to play. At seventeen years old he had manfully shouldered his part—and played it well. A life of selfless valor marked his twenty short years.

Boots had given all. Jim now realized that he also had

Grave of Ernest Boots Thomas

a responsibility to fulfill. Unlike Boots, Jim had survived the war. He was happily married and was starting a family. Now it was his turn to play his part. Just as Sergeant Boots Thomas had given his life for his family, his home, and the generations to come, so Jim recognized that he too had a solemn charge: he had the duty of passing on the history and legacy of Boots Thomas to the next generation.

The tale of Boots' short life appeared to be a tragic one. But to Jim Sledge, who had lost his father at nine years old, tragedy was no stranger. He knew tragedy, and he had learned to meet it with contentment. "God has a purpose," he always explained. "He works providentially in our lives."[58]   This understanding now gave him the strength necessary to devote himself to preserving the history of his boyhood friend.

For years Jim quietly labored to keep Boots' memory alive in his hometown. Others in Monticello joined him, and soon a memorial was erected to honor the memory of Boots Thomas. Jim was overjoyed at having a memorial dedicated to his friend, and he devoted himself to taking care of the monument and the grounds surrounding it. He planted flowers beside the memorial and gladly told the story of Boots Thomas to anyone who stopped by.

As the years passed Jim continued to share Boots' story with generations of young people. Pulling out boxes of photos from his childhood, Jim found pictures of himself and Boots in high school, snapshots Boots had taken on top of the water tower that summer so long ago, and photographs of the two boys just before Boots left for college in 1941. Jim shared the pictures and told the stories to youngsters who had never heard of Boots. As decade followed decade each new generation of children heard the tales and saw the pictures. Amazed, they listened as Jim described the battle of Iwo Jima and showed them photographs of Boots with his men on top of Mount Suribachi.

Whenever he was given an opportunity, Jim was glad to talk about his friend and pass on his legacy to others. Many

Jim Sledge at the Ernest Boots Thomas Memorial
(Boots is pictured over Jim's left shoulder)

people were surprised that Jim spent so much time preserving his friend's memory, but Jim simply replied: "Anybody would have done it for a friend."[59]

Over seventy years now separate Boots' death from the present. Monticello is still a small, rural community, but many things have changed in the quiet little town and around the world. Yet, despite the passage of time, one thing remains the same: the memory of young Boots Thomas and the sacrifice he gave in laying down his life for his family is still known and honored to this day.

But why? Why hasn't his name been forgotten? Why has his memory remained unchanged throughout these many, many years? This is due to the labors of Jim Sledge and others like him. In 1945 Boots gave his life for his family and homeland, and for the seventy years since then his best friend Jim has been giving *his* life for Boots. "Greater love has no man than this." Though Jim Sledge is even now in his nineties, nothing will keep him from honoring the memory of his friend.

Without Jim's efforts, the life and history of Boots Thomas might have quickly become forgotten as the older generation and those who knew him died away. Young people and a new generation of Americans might have never heard of Boots if it hadn't been for him. Jack Thomas, Boots' brother, realized that Jim was responsible for this, and thanked him for it. "If it wasn't for Jim," he explained, "this would have died down with Boots. Jim was a workhorse; he kept things alive!" Because of Jim's actions Jack could truthfully say "Jim Sledge was as good a friend as Boots Thomas ever had."[60]

Jim's simple actions and his untiring labors to keep Boots' memory alive often go unnoticed. This is because Jim doesn't try to draw attention to himself. Instead he devotes his time to explaining to young and old alike the mysterious and wonderful workings of God's providence in the history of Boots Thomas' short life. Jim doesn't want to be noticed. All

Jack Thomas thanks Jim for everything he's done for Boots

he wants is to honor the memory of his fallen friend.

When Boots Thomas helped raise the flag on Iwo Jima he was catapulted into national fame overnight. Boots hadn't tried to become famous and he knew that he didn't deserve the fame any more than anyone else. In the same way Jim Sledge has quietly labored for his entire life to do what he knows is the right thing to do, even if he never gets noticed for it. His selfless dedication to preserving his friend's memory for over seven decades beautifully captures the truth of Solomon's words: "there is a friend who sticks closer than a brother" (Prov. 18:24). Even though he may be an invisible hero, Jim is a true hero indeed.

> *"O God, You have taught me from my youth; and to*
> *this day I declare Your wondrous works. Now also*
> *when I am old and grayheaded, O God, do not forsake*
> *me, until I declare Your strength to this generation,*
> *Your power to everyone who is to come."*
> *— Psalm 71:17-18*

ENDNOTES

1. Monticello News, August 3, 1934.

2. Francis Trevelyan Miller, *History of World War II* (The John C. Winston Company, Philadelphia, 1945), page 63.

3. Ernest I. Thomas, Jr. to Mrs. E. I. Thomas, November 19, 1941. Ernest Boots Thomas Papers, Coll. #98.0009. The Institute on World War II and the Human Experience, Florida State University, Tallahassee, FL.

4. Ernest I. Thomas, Jr. to Mrs. E. I. Thomas, October, 1941. *Ibid.*

5. Ernest I. Thomas, Jr. to Mrs. E. I. Thomas, March 10, 1942. *Ibid.* Wording in this quote has been slightly altered for ease of comprehension. The original text reads: "I do every bit of my homework every night. . . . they don't check on it."

6. Ernest I. Thomas, Jr. to Mrs. E. I. Thomas, October 1, 1941. *Ibid.*

7. Quoted in *Sunday News-Democrat* (Tallahassee, Florida), February 25, 1945, page 8. Original quote begins: "I've got to go, even if I am only 17 . . ."

8. Ernest I. Thomas, Jr. to Mrs. E. I. Thomas, January 8, 1942. *Ibid.*

9. General Jonathan M. Wainwright, *General Wainwright's Story* (Greenwood Press, Publishers, Westport, Connecticut, 1970), page 122.

10. Ernest I. Thomas, Jr. to Mrs. E. I. Thomas, June 4, 1942. Thomas Papers. Institute on WWII, FSU.

11. Ernest I. Thomas, Jr. to Mrs. E. I. Thomas, June 4, 1942. *Ibid.*

12. E. I. Thomas, Jr. to Mrs. E. I. Thomas, June 23, 1942. *Ibid.*

13. E. I. Thomas, Jr. to Mrs. E. I. Thomas, July 1, 1942. *Ibid.*

14. E. I. Thomas, Jr. to Mrs. E. I. Thomas, July 1, 1942. *Ibid.*

15. E. I. Thomas, Jr. to Mrs. E. I. Thomas, July 27, 1942. *Ibid.*

16. E. I. Thomas, Jr. to Mrs. E. I. Thomas, August 13, 1942. *Ibid.*

17. *Ibid.*

18. Major General Fred Haynes (USNC-Ret) and James A. Warren, *The Lions of Iwo Jima: The Story of Combat Team 28 and the bloodiest battle in Marine Corps history* (Henry Holt and Company,

LLC, New York, 2008), page 21.

19. Ernest I. Thomas, Jr. to Mrs. E. I. Thomas, postmarked October 26, 1942. Thomas Papers. Institute on World War II, FSU.

20. E. I. Thomas, Jr. to Mrs. E. I. Thomas, postmarked December 11, 1942. *Ibid.*

21. E. I. Thomas, Jr. to Mrs. E. I. Thomas, January 8, 1943. *Ibid.*

22. General Holland M. Smith, USMC-R, *The Development of Amphibious Tactics in the U.S. Navy* (Marine Corps Historical Center, Washington, D.C., 1992), page vi.

23. E. I. Thomas, Jr. to Mrs. E. I. Thomas, postmarked January 18, 1944. Thomas Papers. Institute on WWII, FSU.

24. E. I. Thomas, Jr. to Mrs. E. I. Thomas, February 16, 1944. *Ibid.*

25. E. I. Thomas, Jr. to Mrs. Thomas, postmarked February 11, 1944. *Ibid.*

26. E. I. Thomas, Jr. to Mrs. Thomas, February 21, 1944. *Ibid.*

27. E. I. Thomas, Jr. to Mrs. Thomas, February 27, 1944. *Ibid.*

28. Richard Wheeler, *The Bloody Battle for Suribachi* (Bluejacket Books, 1994), page 9.

29. Richard Wheeler, *Iwo* (Lippincott & Crowell, New York, 1980), page 55.

30. Letter of Colonel Dave E. Severance, USMC (Ret), to author, March 26, 2014.

31. Letter of Colonel Severance to Pat Smith, May 2, 1978.

32. Ernest I. Thomas, Jr. to Mrs. E. I. Thomas, postmarked September 29, 1944. Thomas Papers. Institute on WWII, FSU.

33. Yoshitaka Horie, *The Memoirs of Fighting Spirit: Major Yoshitaka Horie and the Battle of Iwo Jima* (eds. Robert D. Eldridge and Charles W. Tatum, Naval Institute Press, Annapolis, Maryland, 2011), page 110.

34. Richard Newcomb, *Iwo Jima* (Bantam Books, 1982), page 64.

35. Holland M. Smith and Percy Finch, *Coral and Brass* (Charles Scribner's Sons, New York, 1949), page 254.

36. Lt. John Keith Wells, *Give Me Fifty Marines Not Afraid to Die* (Quality Publications, 1995), page 202.

37. *Charleston Gazette* (Charleston, West Virginia), February 27, 1945, page 5.

38. Wheeler, *The Bloody Battle for Suribachi*, page 124.

39. Letter of Captain Dave E. Severance to Mrs. Ernest Thomas, April 16th, 1945. Courtesy Sledge family.

40. Patrick K. O'Donnell, *Into the Rising Sun* (The Free Press, 2002), page 234.

41. Transcript of interview of Don Pryor and Sergeant Ernest Thomas, February 28, 1945. Courtesy Sledge family.

42. *Ibid.*

43. *Ibid.*

44. O'Donnell, *Into the Rising Sun,* page 66.

45. Transcript of interview of Don Pryor and Sergeant Ernest Thomas, February 28, 1945.

46. *Ibid.*

47. Letter of Don Pryor to Mrs. Ernest Thomas, 1945.

48. Mrs. Ernest Thomas to Ernest I. Thomas, Jr., February 20, 1945. Courtesy Sledge family.

49. *The Daily Democrat,* February 25, 1945, page 1.

50. *Ibid.*

51. Mrs. Thomas to Ernest I. Thomas, Jr., February 25, 1945. Thomas Papers. Institute on WWII, FSU.

52. V-Mail from Jim Sledge to Ernest Thomas, Jr., February 28th, 1945. Courtesy Sledge family.

53. Wheeler, *Iwo,* page 186.

54. Larry Smith, *Iwo Jima* (W. W. Norton & Company, New York, 2008), page 206.

55. *The Monticello News,* April 6, 1945.

56. Western Union telegram to Mrs. Martha T. Thomas, March 28, 11:06 A.M. Courtesy Sledge family.

57. Dr. James Sledge interview with author, November 16, 2015.

58. *Ibid.*, September 27, 2013.

59. *Ibid.*

60. Jack Thomas interview with author, October 19, 2013.

Made in the USA
Middletown, DE
16 September 2018